YOUR KNOWLEDGE HAS VALUE

Bibliographic information published by the German National Library:

The German National Library lists this publication in the National Bibliography; detailed bibliographic data are available on the Internet at http://dnb.dnb.de .

Imprint:

Copyright © 2001 GRIN Verlag, Open Publishing GmbH
Print and binding: Books on Demand GmbH, Norderstedt Germany
ISBN: 9783668264540

This book at GRIN:

http://www.grin.com/en/e-book/323219/application-of-ieee-802-1x-in-hiperlan-type-2

Amleset Kelati

Application of IEEE 802.1X in HiperLAN type 2

GRIN Publishing

GRIN - Your knowledge has value

Since its foundation in 1998, GRIN has specialized in publishing academic texts by students, college teachers and other academics as e-book and printed book. The website www.grin.com is an ideal platform for presenting term papers, final papers, scientific essays, dissertations and specialist books.

Visit us on the internet:

http://www.grin.com/

http://www.facebook.com/grincom

http://www.twitter.com/grin_com

Application of IEEE 802.1X in HiperLAN type 2

Chalmers University of Technology, Department of Signals and Systems
Göteborg, Sweden
Wireless LAN Systems, Ericsson Enterprise AB, Sundbyberg,
Sweden

Master of Science Thesis

July 2001

EX031/2001

By: Amlese Ketlati

Abstract

The research within Information Technology has been subject to a tremendous speed-up in the latest years, mainly due to the reduced prices of the related technology and, consequently, to a strongly increased interest of the users. This causes a positive feedback loop, since many companies decide to invest more money in such area, reducing further the prices and accelerating this process.
One of the major issues in this big race has been the concept *"Be connected always and everywhere"*, which translated in an increased development of public networks on one side and in a further growth of big corporation networks on the other side. The common factors of these big areas are mobility, which implies wireless networks, and availability of services, which also means access to more or less important information.
Increased size, mobility and availability of services on networks that become bigger and bigger increases tremendously the importance of data-security. Trust, authentication, and authorization have become vital key words within the design of big, mobile networks.
IEEE 802.1X, also known as **"Port Based Network Access Control"** is a means for providing authentication and authorization for big networks that offer the possibility to many devices to attach to them, making their services available.
This master thesis work, carried out at *Ericsson Enterprise AB, Wireless LAN Systems* in Sundbyberg (Sweden), had as a primary objective to study the authentication and authorization standard IEEE 802.1X (Draft version 11, released March 27th 2001) and its integration in HIPERLAN type 2 (HIPERLAN/2), which is a standard for wireless LAN. The project has been accomplished for the *Department of Signals and Systems* at the *Chalmers University of Technology in Göteborg, Sweden.* The goals of the thesis work were to analyze the current version of the standards and other related protocols in order to gain competence in the area of the study how IEEE 802.1x could be integrated in HIPERLAN/2 based network. In this work we propose a solution for the implementations problem and design, develop and test a basic prototype.
The result shows that IEEE 802.1x can be deployed within a wireless network based on HIPERLAN/2 by adapting certain features of the two standards and by adopting certain rationale while developing an architecture based on them.

This report is structured in such a way to mirror the different goals of the thesis.

Part 1: Contains a description of the current version of the standard and of other related protocols that collaborate and participate in enhancing security in a typical LAN environment.

Part 2: Illustrates the methodology that has been used and the achieved results in order to integrate IEEE 802.1X and an HIPERLAN/2-based network.

Part 3: Describes roughly the implementation of the prototype, its limitations and further work to make it usable in a professional and non-experimental environment; furthermore, it describes the result of the testing operation.

Part 4: Concludes the report by summarizing the whole work, by illustrating the achieved results and by giving some suggestions for a follow-up of this thesis work.

Acknowledgement

I am very much grateful to my supervisor Yi Cheng at Ericsson Enterprise AB for her valuable consultation and support throughout this thesis work.

I would also like to sincerely thank my examiner at Chalmers, Prof. Arne Svensoon.

I take this opportunity to express my sincere thanks to:

Associate Prof. Eric Ström, Program Director Digital Communication and Systems Technology at Chalmers, for his administrative help, his directions, for the opportunity he gave me to continue my studies and to join Ericsson for my degree project.

Ann-Marie Danielsson Alatalo, Study Counsellor of Electrical and Computer Engineering at Chalmers University of Technology, who encouraged me with her advice and guidance through out my studies at Chalmers including here her frequent follow up.

Mikael Larsson, for the administrative help he gave me at Ericsson Enterprise AB.

Marco Casole, my partner in this thesis project at Ericsson Wireless LAN Systems, for his significant help in understanding many security issues and his co-operation in many aspects through out the project.

As well as all people at Ericsson Enterprise, Wireless LAN Department, that helped me in many practical matters.

Finally, very special thanks to Alem Tekeste, my husband who has been always supporting my choices; and to my sweet son Yonathan who has made his personal sacrifices on his own way.

Table of contents

PART 1: IEEE 802.1X and related protocols

The basic understanding of the concepts of this thesis project are described in this part of the report.

- Chapter 1:   States a short introduction
- Chapter 2:   The basic concepts concerning HIPERLAN 2 are illustrated
- Chapter 3:   Describes the IEEE 802.1X standard
- Chapter 4:   Deals with the Extensible Authentication Protocol (EAP), which is a fundamental part of the IEEE 802.1X standard and with two of its extensions, EAP-TLS and EAP-GSS.
- Chapter 5:   A brief description of RADIUS is given, with particular emphasis on the extensions that allow the use of EAP within RADIUS.

1 Introduction

This chapter aims to give a general overview of the topics of this master thesis, which are wireless LANs, security, and their integration. Furthermore, the last two Sections will depict how the project has been developed, which results have been achieved, and in which environment it will fit.

1.1 Wireless LANs

A Wireless local area network (WLAN) is a flexible data communication system implemented as an extension to or as an alternative for a wired LAN. Using radio frequency (RF) technology, wireless LANs transmit and receive data over air, minimizing the need for wired connection. Thus, wireless LANs combine data connectivity with user mobility.

Wireless LANs have gained strong popularity in a number of vertical markets, including health-care, retail, manufacturing, warehousing, and academia. These industries have profited from the productivity gains of using hand-held terminals and notebook computers to transmit real-time information to centralized hosts for processing. Today's wireless LANs is becoming more widely recognized as a general-purpose connectivity alternative for a broad range of business customers.

A WLAN connects users within a local area, which might be a building or campus, using radio signals to send data. The basic issues, which differentiate WLANs from telephone cellular networks or satellite networks, are frequencies, data rates, coverage area and legal issues. The emphasis of the wireless LANs environments is driven by the strong efforts spent by companies in order to improve data rates, reliability, and quality of service of such networks. Current available standards have data rates up to 11 Mb/s; there are other standards, such as 802.11a and HiperLan2, which will reach data rates up to 54 Mb/s and products based on them are in a development phase. The standardization and availability of such networks will easily pave the way to their adoption and wide spreading.

The possibility to use such networks without having any cable to connect to a plug and the increased user mobility will definitely encourage its use by corporations and public place administrators.

The following list describes some of the many applications of wireless LANs:

- **Corporate**
  With a wireless LAN, corporate employees can take advantage of mobile networking for e-mail, file sharing, and web browsing regardless of where they are in the office.
- **Education**
  Academic institutions leverage the benefits of mobile connectivity be enabling users with notebook computers to connect to the university network for collaborative class discussions and to the Internet for e-mail and web browsing.
- **Finance**
  By carrying a handheld PC with a wireless LAN adapter, financial traders can receive pricing information from a database in real-time and improve the speed and quality of trades. Accounting audit teams increase productivity with quick network setup.
- **Healthcare**
  Using wireless handheld computers to access real-time information, healthcare providers increase productivity and quality of patient care by eliminating patient treatment delays, redundant paperwork, potential transcription errors, and billing cycle delays.
- **Hospitality and Retail**
  Hospitality services can use wireless LANs to directly enter and send food orders from the table. Retail stores can use wireless LANs to set up temporary registers for special events.
- **Manufacturing**
  Wireless networking helps link factory floor workstations and data collection devices to a company's network.
- **Warehousing**
  In warehouses, handheld and forklift-mounted data terminals with barcode readers and wireless data links are used to enter and maintain the location of pallets and boxes. Wireless improves inventory tracking and reduces the costs of physical inventory counts.

Wireless networks may even be used in so-called *ad-hoc networks*, where no central entity provides for access control or authentication. Usually one entity may be elected as a traffic controller or a resource manager. Examples may be in conference rooms, where participants want to exchange information, or home environments, in order to achieve as sometimes addressed as "the wired home" or the "connected home".

1.2 Security

Nowadays Security becomes a very important issue. One consequence is that many existing protocols, which were not originally endowed with security facilities, have now been added with further protocol layers and add-ons, in order to allow their use in hostile environments.

The expansion of open networks, such as the Internet, makes data communications more subject to threats; the probability of an attack grows as the importance and the amount of data travelling on networks increases.

Security is today mainly perceived as a feature, which endow higher-level protocols with, although sometimes it is required to protect communication on the lower level.

Security services on high-level protocols imply a bigger awareness of the user and the necessity to adapt applications. On the other hand a finer granularity can be obtained, up to be able to protect data on a per-document basis, such adapting the cost of the security algorithm to the actual value of the data being transmitted. Furthermore, the protection is ensured from source to destination, thus obtaining an end-to-end protection.

IEEE 802.1X, which is one of the main topics of this thesis, defines a protocol to achieve authentication before allowing access to network services. The authentication occurs at the first point of attachment to a LAN and not somewhere in the core of it. This has implication in terms of increased security, reduced complexity, greater scalability and availability.

Security is a common and very important issue of wireless LAN; users perceive a connection without wires as particularly unsecured, although the real difference from normal wired networks lies at the physical layer. As previously hinted at, the medium through which a WLAN sends data is the air, which means that it has non-defined boundaries and that it is unprotected from outside signals. These features lead basically to two kinds of attack, which are typical of the wireless medium.

Eavesdropping is a kind of *passive* attack that consists in listening to the communication that is happening on the medium. Because there are no real boundaries of the wireless medium, this kind of attack can be easily performed by having a transceiver, which is able to demodulate correctly the signals being transmitted on the network. This kind of attack can be avoided by using particular kinds of modulations (**Frequency Hopping Spread Spectrum** or **Dynamic Selection Spread Spectrum**) which make the attacker need to know other parameters than the transmission frequency, or by encrypting the session.

Denial of service is a kind of *active* attack that aims to prevent a user to have access to certain or all services. It can be achieved in several ways; on the physical level, it consists in sending burst of signals with no meaning. This prevents users to send signals, since the medium results busy, or to understand the signals being sent.

1.3 Methodology and achieved results for the thesis work

The thesis work has gone through different stages, which were necessary in order to achieve the goal that has been proposed. The whole work started with an intensive study work, whose aim was to gain a deep knowledge of the subject. This was necessary to pass to the next stage and to create a competence in the area, which was actually one of the main goals of the master thesis.

After this preliminary study-phase, the second goal was to propose a model of integration between IEEE 802.1X and HIPERLAN/2. The basic question that needed an answer was: "How can a network, based on the HIPERLAN/2 standard, use IEEE 802.1X to perform authentication and access control". In order to provide for a solution to this problem the following aspects have been considered:

- How these two standards integrate on a protocol point of view.
- How the operation of the HIPERLAN/2 standard needs to be modified or adapted in order to be used with IEEE 802.1X.
- How a protocol exchange can look like and which authentication methods could be used.

- What the requirements and the possible software architecture for a complete implementation are.

Part 2 of the report illustrates how these aspects have been analyzed and what kind of solution has been proposed for each of those problems.

The next step was to build a prototype of the IEEE 802.1X standard, in order to evaluate its feasibility and how it can be deployed in a complete environment. Unfortunately, there are no HIPERLAN/2 complete product available on the market and it was therefore necessary to implement the prototype on a different kind of network. Many of the conclusions of the previous step were nonetheless still applicable. The prototype was then tested in a complete environment: the basic protocol exchange was tried out and some other additional features were added. Part 3 describes and summarizes the work that has been done.

Part 4 of this report depicts the conclusions that might be drawn from the thesis and tries to outline some basic concepts that result form the whole project. Furthermore, it gives some guidelines for continuing the work that has started here.

1.4 Typical operational environment

IEEE 802.1X was designed in order to provide a means of authenticating devices being attached to a port of a network access point and willing to have access to the network infrastructure services. Typically, this is needed in environments where the access to the network is publicly available, or within networks with many point of attachments, thus making it difficult to check each of them without having any precise security and administration policy. Such environments may be big corporations' LANs, possibly with areas where the network is publicly available, technology or business parks, conference rooms, airports or train stations, malls, and even some open-air environments with public network access.

The focus of this thesis is a business wireless environment with a relatively high number of points of attachments but no public access. An example of this is given in Figure 1.

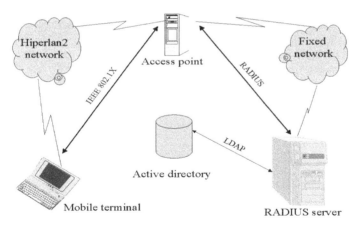

Figure 1: A typical operating environment.

The corporate network is mainly based on a fixed Ethernet network, fully or almost fully switched. Within this network it is possible to have wireless access through some wireless protocol, let's say HiperLAN2. The access points to the wireless network are connected to the fixed network and act as bridges to it. They are therefore endowed at least with the **Ethernet Service Specific Convergence Sublayer (SSCL)** [HL2ETSSCL] in order to match different kind of services and adapt PDUs of the different networks. Each mobile terminal will be identified, within the global corporation network, by its 48 bits IEEE MAC address, while within the HiperLAN2 segment it will be only addressed by its 8 bits MAC ID.

The authentication of the mobile terminals in order to grant them access to the network resources will be achieved through IEEE 802.1X. The authentication server will be a RADIUS server located on the fixed network and accessible through it. In order to get information, the RADIUS server will have access to a WINDOWS 2000 **Active Directory** through the **Lightweight Directory Access Protocol (LDAP)**. Mobile terminals will be based on Windows 98, Windows 98 Second Edition or Windows 2000 Professional as operating systems. Servers on the network will be based on Windows 2000 Server or on Windows NT 4 as operating system. The business environment now described is mainly characterized by the following features:

- Host can access all or almost all resources locally available.
- No charging is required.
- Hosts are subject to administration and management.
- The environment can be assigned a certain level of trust.
- Key and certificate distribution is not so difficult.

This environment can somehow be considered as experimental, since the Windows 2000 based environments are still on a way to be better defined and it is still not possible, at the current time, to have a complete working HiperLAN2-based network.

Figure 2 provides another view of the described environment.

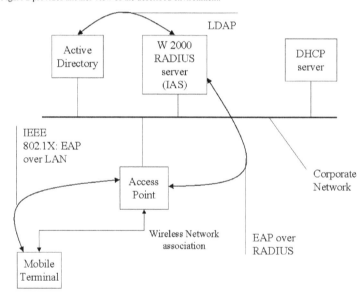

Figure 2: A working operative environment.

To summarize, the focus of the thesis is business environment with wireless access to the network. The deployed wireless standard will be HIPERLAN/2 in the business configuration ([HL2BUE]), which means configured to work in the **centralized mode**, i.e. with Access Points controlling the communication, allowing the flow of packets to the wired network and allocating resources. Authentication and access control will be based on IEEE 802.1X; the Access Points will act as RADIUS clients, while the RADIUS server will be placed on the fixed network. It will likely be a Windows 2000 Server machine; acting as **Internet Access Server (IAS)**, which incorporates a RADIUS server. The RADIUS server will retrieve user and access information from a Windows 2000 Active Directory.

2 HIPERLAN 2

The *European Telecommunications Standards Institute (ETSI)* has started the *Broadband Radio Access Network (BRAN)* project, which aims to develop a set of standard for broadband wireless networks. The categories of systems covered by the BRAN project are summarized as follows:

- The first result of this project was a standard called *High Performance Radio Local –Area Network, type 1 (HIPERLAN 1)* are compatible with wired LANs based on Ethernet and Token Ring standards. This system is intended to be operated in the 5GHz band.
- The following standard was HIPERLAN 2, which provides high speed radio communications system with typical data rate from 6 MHz to 54 Mbits /s. It can access to different broad-band core networks and moving terminals, with QoS support.
- The recent projects, which have planned but not started yet, are HIPERACCESS, which will provide outdoor, high speed (25 Mb/s), fixed radio access, and HIPERLINK, which will provide extremely high-speed (up to 155 Mb/s) radio links for static interconnections.

2.1 Overview

The standardization activity of HIPERLAN 2 gave its first result in 1999. HIPERLAN 2 [HL2OV] operates within the 5 GHz spectrum, in Europe it will be placed in the ranges between 5.15 and 5.30 GHz, and between 5.470 and 5.725, for a 455 MHz wide spectrum. In USA and Japan, it will be allocated different intervals, according to local policy rules.

The topology of a typical HIPERLAN 2 based network is illustrated in Figure 3, it has **Access Points (APs)**, which provide for access to the wireless network, and **Mobile Terminals (MTs)**, which are the devices willing to have access to the network. The APs will typically be attached to a fixed network. This operating way is called **centralized mode** since all traffic passes through the access point, even if it is directed from one MT to another MT that is connected to the same AP. The AP is in charge of allocating resources, giving access to a fixed network, and other administrative tasks. All MTs, before operating, need to establish an **association** with an AP, in order to be allowed to operate on the HIPERLAN 2 network; an association procedure consists of link and capabilities negotiation, and of the establishment of user connections. In order to start to send and receive data, it is necessary to open a **DLC user connection (DUC)**, which defines the features of the data transfer.

It may happen that there is no AP in charge with providing access to a fixed network. In this situation the network will operate in **direct mode**; the communication between MTs will occur directly from the source to the destination MT, but there is still need of a **Central Controller (CC)** in charge with allocating resources to the terminals. The result will be an *ad-hoc* network, whose applications vary form home-environments to military infrastructures.

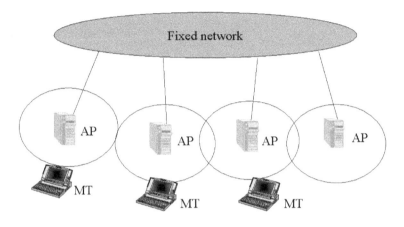

Figure 3: HIPERLAN 2 centralized mode.

2.2 Protocol architecture

The HIPERLAN 2 protocol has three basic layers. It defines a **Physical layer (PHY)**, with the same semantic of the ISO/OSI layer, while the link level is constituted by different sublayers: the **Data Link Control (DLC)** layer and the **Convergence Layer (CL)**, which is in charge with providing interoperability with different higher layers (HL) or link layers. The whole protocol stack can be considered divided vertically in two parts: a **control plane** part, for administrative and control operations, and a **user plane** part, for the transmission of traffic over the established connections. A complete view is given in Figure 4.
The DLC layer, in charge with functions for medium access and transmission as well as connection handling, is made up of a set of sublayers:

- **Medium Access Control (MAC)** protocol.
- **Error Control (EC)** protocol
- **Radio Link Control (RLC)** protocol with the associated signaling entities **DLC Connection Control (DCC)**, the **Radio Resource Control (RRC)** and the **Association Control Function (ACF)**.

The MAC protocol and the EC protocol constitute the basic data transport functions for the DLC layer.

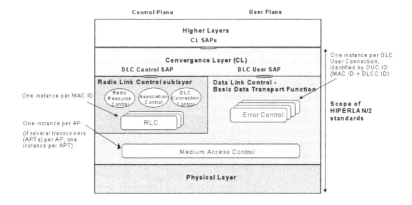

Figure 4: HIPERLAN 2 protocol Stack (Source: [HL2DLC]).

2.2.1 The Physical layer

OFDM, the modulation scheme chosen for the HIPERLAN 2 [HL2PHY] standard is very effective in high dispersive environments. The different channels, each of them assigned automatically and dynamically to an AP, are 20 MHz wide. Each channel is further divided into 52 subcarriers; 48 of them are actually used to carry data while the other four are pilots, which facilitate phase tracking for coherent demodulation.
The entire bit stream coming from the upper level is divided into different parallel interleaved bit streams and each of them will modulate a subcarrier of a channel. Within a channel, many modulation schemes are possible, such as Binary Phase-Shift Keying (BPSK), Quadrature Phase-Shift keying (QPSK), and Quadrature Amplitude Modulation (QAM), up to 64 QAM, which provides for the maximum data rate of 54 MB/s. A modulation scheme is chosen according to what has been negotiated in the association phase and to local radio conditions. OFDM allows a very robust transmission but needs a well-designed system.

2.2.2 The DLC layer: basic data transport function

The basic data transport functions of the DLC layer [HL2DLC] are made up of the MAC protocol and the EC protocol. As previously hinted, they both have a user panal and a control panal for simple data transmission functions and control functions.
The Medium Access Control (MAC) protocol is in charge of regulating the access to the air interface. The air interface is based on **Time-Division Duplex (TDD)** and **Time-Division Multiple Access (TDMA)**. This means that within the same time frame, multiple communications are allowed in both downlink (from the AP to the MTs) and uplink (from the MTs to the APs) directions. Time slots are allowed dynamically depending on the current traffic load and different requirements for each connection. Within an HIPERLAN 2 network, an MT is identified uniquely in each cell, i.e. in the area covered by one AP, by its MAC ID, assigned at association time and whose scope is limited to each AP. Since an AP will usually act as a bridge

to a fixed network, an MT is likely to be identified by an IEEE MAC address within this broader scope. On higher levels, an MT is likely to be identified by an IP address, and hence mobility issues should be considered as well, especially in handovers, i.e. the operation of association to another AP. In case of multicast data transfer there are two ways to handle this situation: **N-Multicast**, where it is dealt as N unicast connection, with good reliability but bad bandwidth consumption, or **MAC Multicast**, where a MAC ID is assigned to each multicast group, saving bandwidth but loosing reliability.

The basic MAC frame structure on the air interface has a fixed duration of 2 ms, repeated every time, and comprises different phases, i.e. part of the frame are devoted to different uses, with fixed or variable length. The **Broadcast phase (BC)** contains information broadcast to all MTs associated with that AP; the **Downlink phase (DL)** transports data from the AP to the MTs, while the **Uplink phase (UL)** is used for data transfer from the MTs to the AP. If direct mode is available, a **Direct phase (DiL)** is inserted between DL and UL. At the end of the MAC frame, the **Random phase (RA)** is used by the MT to ask for resources or to start a new association. It is the only phase where contention is possible. Figure 5 depicts the MAC frame.

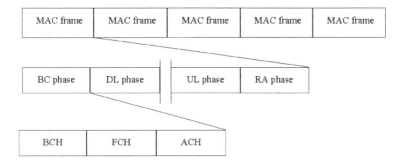

Figure 5: HIPERLAN 2 MAC frame (Source: [HL2DLC]).

The DL, DiL and UL phases consist of two types of Protocol Data Units (PDUs): long PDUs and short PDUs. Long PDUs have a fixed size of 54 bytes and contain user data and control data. Short PDUs are 9 bytes long and contain only control data.

Within the different phases, the HIPERLAN 2 standard places the so-called **transport channels**, which describe the basic message format. They are used to carry different kinds of data, depending on the **logical channels**, which are mapped onto them.

A **logical channel** is any distinct path of data; a set of logical channel is defined for different kinds of data transfer services as offered by the MAC entity. Each logical channel is defined by the type of information it carries and the interpretation of the values in the corresponding messages. A logical channel can be considered to operate between logical connections end points and, hence, between logical entities.

The following transport channels are defined:

- **Broadcast Channel (BCH)**. It conveys control information (about transmission power, starting and finishing point of the FCH and RCH (see next paragraph), and identifiers) directed to all MTs.
- **Frame Channel (FCH)**. Contains an exact description of how resources have been allocated within the current MAC frame.
- **Access Feedback Channel (ACH)**. Conveys information on previous access attempts to the RCH.
- **Long Transport Channel (LCH)**. Is used to transport user data that is sent as unicast, multicast or broadcast data, and signaling information for the user connection. Contains long PDUs.
- **Short Transport Channel (SCH)**. Transports control information encapsulated in short PDUs.

- **Random Channel (RCH)**. It is used by the MTs to request transmission resources. It is the only channel where contention is possible. An MT sends a **Resource Request (RR)** indicating how much and what kind of data it needs to transmit.

The following logical channels have been defined:

- **Broadcast Control Channel (BCCH)**. Contains broadcast control channel information concerning the whole radio cell. Used for sending identifiers of the AP and the net and other information that sometimes is used as beacon.
- **Frame Control Channel (FCCH)**. Describes exactly how resources are allocated within the current frame.
- **Random Access Feedback Channel (RFCH)**. The purpose is to inform those MTs that have used the RCH in the previous frame, about their result of their access attempts. Resources are granted by the AP through **Resource Grants (RGs)**.
- **RLC Broadcast Channel (RBCH)**. Contains broadcast control information concerning the whole cell. It is used to transmit broadcast RLC messages, a MAC ID to a non-associated terminal and convergence layer information.
- **Dedicated Control Channel (DCCH)**. Contains signaling information needed for the user connection and can be used both in the uplink and in the downlink phase. It is established implicitly during the establishment of an association.
- **User Broadcast Channel (UBCH)**. Carries user data coming from the upper convergence layer but directed to all MTs of a cell.
- **User Multicast Channel (UMCH)**. Contains user data coming from the convergence layer, directed to those MTs that joined a multicast group.
- **User Data Channel (UDCH)**. Contains user data directed to an MT.
- **Link Control Channel (LCCH)**. Bi-directional channel used to carry error control messages.
- **Association Control Channel (ASCH)**. Used only to convey information needed for the establishment of a new association.

How the different logical channels are mapped onto transport channels is shown in Figure 6 (downlink) and Figure 7 (uplink).

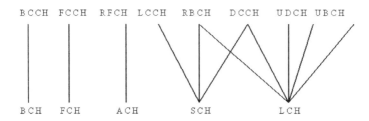

Figure 6: Mapping of logical channel to transport channels (downlink) (Source: [HL2DLC]).

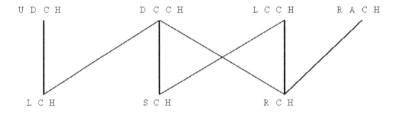

Figure 7: Mapping of logical channels to transport channels (uplink) (Source: [HL2DLC]).

2.2.3 The DLC layer: RLC sublayer

The Radio Link Control (RLC) sublayer [HL2RLC] provides for a transport service for the signaling entities **Association Control Function (ACF)**, **Radio Resource Control function (RRC)**, and the **DLC user connection control function (DCC)**.

Before an MT is allowed to have access to the HIPERLAN 2 network, it must establish an association with the AP or the CC. The MT starts with listening to the BCH of different APs in order to decide where to establish an association, according to the net operator identifier and the best signal. Association requests are conveyed in the **Association Control Channel (ACH)**.

Before starting to transmit traffic, an MT has to establish at least one **DLC user connection (DCC)**. The DCC control signaling is transmitted over the DCCH, in order to control the resources for each MAC entity. The characteristics of each connection may be exchanged during the connection.

The Radio Resource Control (RRC) functions are in charge with the radio link quality operations, which might result in a **handover**, i.e. an association with a new AP with a better radio signal. In order to avoid a complete disassociation and reassociation, HIPERLAN 2 supports the exchange of information over the fixed network in order to minimize the impact of a handover.

The RRC functions deal also with the **Dynamic Frequency Selection (DFS)** algorithm, the **Power Save** features and the **MT Alive** operations, which supervise if an MT is currently inactive.

2.2.4 The packet based convergence layer

In order to allow interoperability with other kinds of network and higher-level protocols, the HIPERLAN 2 standard defines what is called **Convergence Layer (CL)**. A convergence layer has basically two functions:

- To adapt service requests from higher levels or other kinds of networks to those that are available on the HIPERLAN 2 DLC layer.
- To convert the different format of other protocol, of fixed or variable length, into the format accepted by the DLC layer.

The padding, segmentation and reassemble function of the fixed size DLC Service Data Units (SDU) is one key issue that makes it possible to standardize and implement a DLC and a PHY that is independent of the fixed network to which the HIPERLAN 2 network is connected to.

There are currently two convergence layers defined within the HIPERLAN 2 standard, as depicted in Figure 8. The **Cell based CL** aims to provide for an interface towards protocols with fixed size PDUs. An example of this is ATM. The **Packet based CL** provides for an interface towards all those network, which have a variable size PDU. Examples of such networks are UMTS, PPP, Ethernet and IEEE 1394 "Firewire". The architecture of the Packet based convergence layer is depicted in Figure 9.

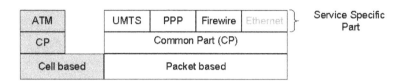

Figure 8: HIPERLAN 2 convergence layers.

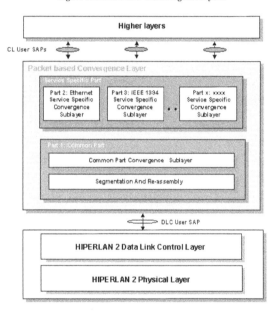

Figure 9: Packet based convergence layer (Source [HL2PBCL]).

The Packet based convergence layer [HL2PBCL] is made up of two parts, a **Common Part** and a **Service Specific Convergence sublayer (SSCS)**. The common part performs the same kinds of operations for every sort of packet based network, while the service specific part is dependant on the overlying network and allows easy adaptation of higher level services to the DLC services.

The common part is further divided into two sublayers: the **Common Part Convergence Sublayer (CPCS)**, and the **Segmentation and RE-assembly (SR)** part.

The function of the CPCS is to take packets received from the overlying SSCS, to add padding and additional information and to pass it to the SR part. It has furthermore to remove and interpret padding and information from the packets received from the underlying level, and passes them to the SSCS.

The SR part takes packets from the CPCS, segments them into fixed size data unit and passes them to the DLC layer; it also performs the reverse operation, taking packets from the DLC, reassembling them and passing them to the CPCS. It performs an in-order delivery of packets for the CPCS.

Following the general HIPERLAN 2 semantic, even the CL is divided vertically into two parts: a *user plane* and a *control plane*, which allow different types of operations.

The Ethernet SSCS [HL2ETSSCS] makes the HIPERLAN 2 look like the segment of a switched Ethernet. Its main functions are to preserve the original frames and to map the services available on an Ethernet-based network to an HIPERLAN 2 network, in terms of QoS and traffic types.

Ethernet SSCS offers basically two different types of QoS:

- The **best effort scheme**, which is mandatory. It is the default QoS type and all traffic is treated in the same way, without any guarantee of QoS parameters.

- The **IEEE 802.1p based priority scheme**, which is optional and separates different types of traffic in different priority queues. There are eight different priority levels, mapped to eight or less, dependant on the system) different system queues. Each queue is then mapped to a DLC user connection (DUC), according to its priority, and, naturally, to its destination MAC addresses. In the Ethernet frame, the priority is indicated by a tag placed after the source and the destination address. In HIPERLAN/2 the Quality of Service parameters are negotiated at association time.

As hinted in the previous paragraph, it is up to the SSCS (control plane) to map the different addresses of the higher level to DUCs of the DLC level, since it is able to identify destination MTs only in this way. The SSCS of the AP is actually different form the MT's SSCS: the latter will send all data to the AP, while the former has to decide whether send data back to the HIPERLAN 2 network or forward it to the fixed Ethernet network.

2.3 HIPERLAN 2 security features

The HIPERLAN 2 standard provides for its own security features, in order to guarantee authentication and confidentiality of the data being exchanged on the air interface. The following Subsections give an overview of how the standard confronts with the security problem.

2.3.1 Key exchange

The key exchange procedure will occur during the association time. It will also happen before authentication, in order to have the identities exchanged during the association procedure.

The exchange of the keys is based on a Diffie-Hellman procedure. The two entities being involved in the protocol, i.e. the AP and the MT, exchange their public DH values and, starting from them, they will work out the keys used for encryption.

The encryption keys, also denoted as **Session Secret Keys (SSKs)**, are valid only for one session, and may be refreshed during one session. They are known only to the AP and the specific MT. In order to exchange encrypted multicast and broadcast data, AP and MTs of the same cell share common keys, univocally identified by an ID. These keys are exchanged first at association time (distributed by the AP) and even during the session in order to refresh them.

2.3.2 Encryption

The HIPERLAN 2 standard considers two different encryption algorithms, which is possible to choose between the DES algorithm and the triple DES algorithm. The encryption keys are derived from operations made on the DH keys exchanged before; the actual encryption operations start as soon as the AP and MT have exchanged and calculated their keys.

In order to increase the effectiveness of the algorithm, HIPERLAN 2 makes use of the **Output FeedBack (OFB)** operation mode (Figure 10), and for this reason an **Initialization Vector (IV)** is needed. The seed for the IVs, i.e. the value starting from which the IVs are generated, are periodically sent to the MTs in the RBCH logical channel, starting from association time as soon as the DH values have been exchanged and before encryption actually starts. To obtain the IVs, a function cycles stepwise in order to produce a set of non-repeating values; every LCH is encrypted with a different IV.

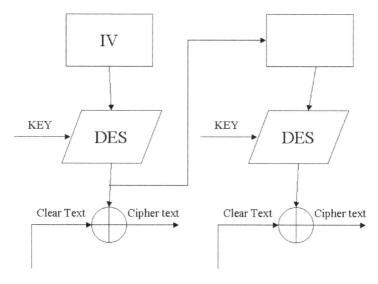

Figure 10: DES OFB mode.

2.3.3 Authentication

The HIPERLAN 2 standard allows two different authentication mechanisms, which are negotiated at association time:

- **Pre-shared key based.**
- **RSA signature based.**

Regardless of the authentication mechanism being used, the scheme is always based on challenge and response. After having decided which mechanism to use at the beginning of the association phase, the MT receives a challenge from the AP, and sends back a response, together with a new challenge, in order to perform mutual authentication. The AP decides about the correctness of the response sent by the MT and works out its response to the received challenge. Then it is the MT's turn to decide whether the AP has successfully authenticated.

In the pre-shared key mechanism, the response is calculated by applying the MD5 algorithm [MD5] and the HMAC [HMAC] algorithm to the authentication string given by the concatenation of the challenge, the DH public values, the list of the proposed authentication/encryption mechanisms and the selected mechanism. The keys being used are pre-shared, long term, authentication key, known both to the AP and to the MT. HIPERLAN 2 does not specify how such keys are distributed between the entities being involved in the authentication procedure. Such keys are not supposed to be transferred on the HIPERLAN 2 network and are not the keys exchanged with the DH procedure, which are used only for encryption. This kind of mechanism suits to environments with a limited number of MTs, without key distribution problems.

The RSA signature based mechanism calculates the challenge as a signature of the authentication string as described in the previous paragraph, using the private key of the entity working out the response. The HIPERLAN 2 standard does not specify which binding should exist between a public key, necessary to decide about the correctness of the signature, and the entity being authenticated. A digital certificate seems to be the best solution, but this will be implementation dependent, since it is not specified how this should happen. There are three different key lengths that are allowed in this mechanism: 512, 768 or 1024 bits.

3. IEEE 802.1X

This chapter gives a detailed description of the IEEE 802.1X Port Based Network Access Control standard, in which the draft in use is the version 11, released on March 27th, 2001.

3.1 General concepts and Architectural framework

The aim of IEEE 802.1X [8021X9], known as **Port based Network Access Control,** is to provide a means of authenticating devices attached to a LAN port, that has point-to-point characteristics, and preventing unauthorized devices to have access to the services available on that network, by making use of the physical access characteristics of IEEE 802 LAN infrastructures. A port is a single point of attachment to the LAN infrastructure.

The typical environment of such a protocol is a *public* LAN infrastructure or a *corporation* LAN, where users can be physically connected or create associations (in case of wireless LANs) thus obtaining access to resources and services, which might be available. *Ad-hoc networks* may also need to perform authentication, in order to determine a trusted network; all entities, in this case, should be able to ask for and perform the authentication function and to be authenticated as well.

The access point to the network, called **Authenticator,** asks the device that is willing to have access to the network services, called the **Supplicant,** to authenticate itself. The authentication function occurs usually in another system, called the **Authentication Server,** likely to be a RADIUS server. The authenticator, i.e. the access point, is not requested to understand the nature of the authentication information exchanged between supplicant and authentication server; it simply controls the state of its port. For additional features like encryption features negotiation and key-exchange, this might be a problem. In certain circumstances, the authenticator must understand the information, which it actually simply forwards to the authentication server during the protocol exchange.

The typical architecture framework of an environment based on IEEE 802.1X may be depicted as in Figure 11.

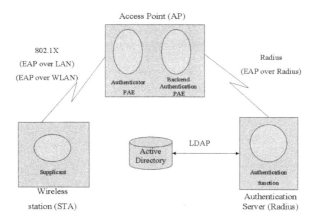

Figure 11: General architecture of an IEEE 802.1X system.

A wireless station, i.e. the supplicant, wishes to use the services offered by a wireless LAN infrastructure through an Access Point (AP), which gives access to the LAN. To achieve this, it creates an association with the AP and asks, or typically will be asked, to perform authentication. The AP will act as an authenticator; i.e. it will be the point where authentication is requested. The authentication function, as previously hinted at, will be performed by an authentication server, which will usually be located on another machine. A typical situation is to have a RADIUS server acting as an authentication server, and the RADIUS server accessing an **Active Directory**, using the **Lightweight Directory Access Protocol (LDAP)** to retrieve information in order to perform the authentication function (using LDAP to access Active Directory for information is a solution for Windows 2000 environments, it cannot be called a typical situation). The authenticator will control the access status of its port basing on the outcome of the authentication process.

The effect of the IEEE 802.1X is to create two distinct points of access to the point of attachment of the authenticator's system, as illustrated in Figure 12 and Figure 13.

- The **uncontrolled port**: Is the point of access, through which PDUs can pass without being blocked; this access point is usually used to transmit authentication information. This is needed since the mobile terminal has not access to the network and it would otherwise be impossible for it to exchange authentication information with the authentication server.

- The **controlled port**: is the second point of access, which allows information to flow through it only when its status is *authorized*.

Both ports are to be considered as part of the same point of attachment; furthermore, any frame received on the physical port will be available on both the controlled and the uncontrolled port.

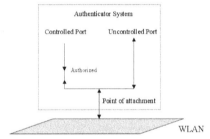

Figure 12: Authorized state (Source: [8021X11]).

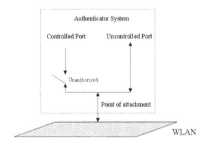

Figure 13: Unauthorized state (Source: [8021X11]).

The controlled port is set to an *unauthorized* state before starting operation, and as soon as a device is attached to the port, the AP asks for authentication. With a successful process, the state of the port will be set to *authorized*. The state of the controlled port can be controlled externally by management operations and can be forced to be unconditionally authorized or unauthorized (that is without considering the result of the authentication function), or can be set according of the outcome of the authentication operations.

The control performed over the frames passing through the port may be executed only for frames flowing in one direction, i.e. incoming frames, or flowing in both directions. This allows relaxing the access control in order to send out diagnostic or management packets. There are different scenarios in which this feature can be quite useful and prevent different facilities to be completely disabled.

3.2 Packet format and Protocol exchange

IEEE 802.1X defines the encapsulation technique that allows to transport Extensible Authentication Protocol (EAP) [EAP] packets between a supplicant and an authenticator through LAN environment. This technique is known as EAP over LAN (EAPOL). In the following description, the encapsulation technique into IEEE 802.3 frames will be described as an example, but other kinds of encapsulation will be quite similar. A typical format of the packet will be like in Figure 14.
There are currently five different types of packets:

- **EAP packet.** This packet encapsulates an EAP packet used to perform authentication.

- **EAPOL-Start packet.** It is sent by the supplicant to indicate that it wishes to be authenticated.

- **EAPOL-Logoff packet.** Sent by supplicant to indicate that it is willing to terminate the current session.
- **EAPOL-Encapsulated-AFS-Alert packet.** Used for traffic like SNMP traps. The format is not defined.
- **EAPOL-Key packet.** Sent by the authenticator to the supplicant in order to send an encryption key.

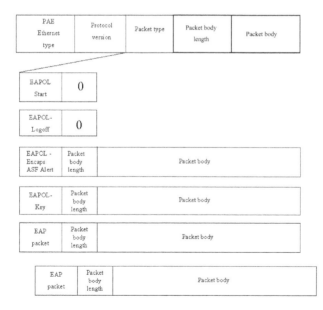

Figure 14: EAPOL packet format.

The **EAPOL-Key** packet contains a descriptor of a key to be used for encryption, authentication or signature. It is used by the authenticator to send information about a key to the supplicant or by the supplicant to send a key to the authenticator.

The format of the **EAP** packet is depicted in Figure 17.

To start the protocol exchange the authenticator will send an **EAP-Request/Identity** packet, and an association is established between a wireless station and an access point. Then the supplicant replies by sending an **EAP-Response/Identity** packet, by which it communicates its credentials to the authenticator. There may be times that the supplicant starts the protocol by sending an **EAPOL-Start** to the authenticator, who then replies with an **EAP-Request/Identity** packet..

The authenticator forwards this packet to the authentication server, usually a RADIUS server, who replies by sending a challenge or by asking the supplicant to provide a password or something else to confirm its identity. This phase is strictly dependent on what authentication mechanism will be used by the entities being involved in the process. The current version of EAP defines three different authentication schemes, MD5 [MD5] challenge, One Time Password [OTP] and Generic Token Card, but it will probably be enhanced with different and stronger mechanism. A typical protocol exchange by using One Time Password is illustrated in Figure 15.

The forwarding task performed by the authenticator, may be either achieved by encapsulating EAP packets into RADIUS packets exploiting the EAP RADIUS extensions (see Chapter 5), or by extracting the information out of the packet and putting them into normal RADIUS attributes. The first solution allows a simplification of the authenticator (or better of the Backend authentication state machine, as depicted in Section 3.5) but needs the RADIUS server to support the EAP-extensions. The second solution needs the authenticator (backend authentication) to extract the information from an EAP-Response packet and to prepare a RADIUS packet, but allows dealing with a normal RADIUS server.

When the supplicant wishes to end the session and close the connection, it sends an **EAPOL-Logoff** packet to signal the authenticator and in this case the port should be set to *unauthorized*, in order to avoid attacks that might be exploit to an open authenticated session.

If the authentication process fails, the authentication server sends an **EAP-Failure** packet to the authenticator, who forwards it to the supplicant and keeps the controlled port in the *unauthorized* state. All the decisions made by the authenticator are based on the outcome of the authenticator server. If the it is the RADIUS server, as it likely to be, the authenticator will look only the RADIUS return code, neglecting the EAP packet that might be included in the response.

Since IEEE 802.1X is to be considered a link-level security protocol, it has to deal with retransmission, as the underlying protocol may not reliably guarantee the deliverance of the frames. IEEE 802.1X states that the authenticator is in charge of the retransmission of frames. If the authenticator does not receive the response to a request it has sent, it must retransmit the request. A supplicant, on the other hand, has to send a response every time it receives a request, even if a response has already been sent. The supplicant retransmits only EAPOL-Start packets. EAPOL-Logoff Packet is never retransmitted. It has to be pointed out that a typical LAN environment has an error-rate that is usually quite low; wireless LAN might indeed have a lower reliability.

It may happen that either the authenticator or the supplicant is not capable of authentication. The protocol has been designed in a way to deal with such situations. If the supplicant does not support authentication it will not respond to the authenticator's EAP-Request/Identity packet; the authenticator will retransmit but the port will never be released. If the authenticator does not support authentication, the supplicant will send EAPOL-Start packets and never receive an answer. After a certain amount of times it has retransmitted its packet, it will assume that the authenticator does not support authentication and starts to send higher level traffic, considering the port set to the authorized state.

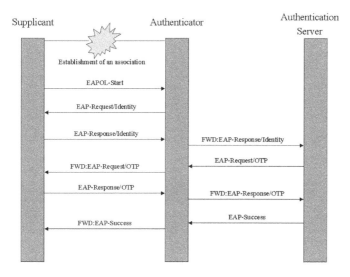

Figure 15: IEEE 802.1X basic protocol exchange.

3.3 Implementation issues

In order to have a clear idea about how the different parts of a security system based on IEEE 802.1X should fit each other, it is worth to define roughly which modules should be present and how they should communicate. Figure 16 depicts this architecture.

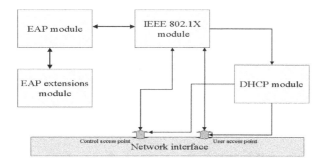

Figure 16: Software architecture.

The **IEEE 802.1X module** sends messages over the network through the *user access point* of the network interface and may set administrative variables through the *control access point*. This is very important in the

---

case of the authenticator, because it needs to have control over the network interface in order to deny access to the supplicant, if authentication fails. It communicates also with the **EAP module** and, indirectly, with the **EAP extensions module**: they will be responsible for the EAP conversation.

The **DHCP module** has access to the network interface and may even be triggered by the IEEE 802.1X module: this is the case that the DHCP module should receive a timeout error message, because authentication took too long and DHCP packets couldn't flow through the network.

This architecture is quite general and can be applied to both the supplicant and the authenticator. The DHCP module needs to be triggered in the supplicant to send a request again, if it has failed because authentication has not yet completed. Furthermore, the IEEE 802.1X needs to have a strong control over the network interface in the case of the authenticator.

The standard specifies nine different state machines that model the behavior of the IEEE 802.1X protocol. Not all of them should be present in a system: it depends on what functionality that system wishes to implement. The state machines are:

- The **Port Timers** state machine.
- The **Authenticator PAE** state machine
- The **Authenticator Key Transmit** state machine
- The **Supplicant Key Transmit** state machine
- The **Reauthentication Timer** state machine
- The **Backend authentication** state machine
- The **Controlled Directions** state machine
- The **Supplicant PAE** state machine
- The **Key Receive** state machine

The *Port Timers* state machine is in charge of decrementing every second their value until they arrive zero. They are set, read, and initialized by the different state machines.

The *Authenticator* state machine's role is to enforce authentication by sending EAP-Request/Identity to the supplicant and to realise the function to set the status of the controlled port according to the outcome of the authentication exchange. It has to perform the access control function.

The *Authenticator Key Transmit* and the *Supplicant Key Transmit* state machines are in charge to send a key to the supplicant or to the authenticator if such a key is available.

The *Reauthentication Timer* state machines is in charge to check if the reauthentication timer expired, which means that the supplicant needs to reauthenticate. This timer is usually set to an initial value of 3600 seconds, but can be set to other values according to local policies.

The *Backend Authentication* state machine is responsible with communicating with the authentication server and is located on the same system as the authenticator state machine. It forwards responses to the authentication server and receives requests from it. Its presence allows the separation of the authentication function from the authenticator.

The *Controlled Directions* state machine is responsible to ensure the correct values of the parameters that regulate if control should be performed only on incoming packets or on packets flowing in both directions. It actually does not make sense to control only outgoing traffic.

The *Supplicant* state machine communicates with the authenticator state machine and waits for a response. It may happen that a supplicant starts to send packets before having received the response of the authentication process. If the access point does not support authentication, this turns out to be a gain of time.

The *Key Receive* state machine is in charge of receiving a key and processing it. The standard does not specify how to process a key. It is system and implementation dependent.

The standard defines a set of managed objects and management functions on such objects. The aim is to provide for facilities that support the planning, organization, supervision, control, protection, and security of communication resources, and account for their use. It also defines a single **Management Information Base (MIB)** module, containing the managed objects, divided into groups, and their relationships with variables, parameters and counters defined together with the state machines.

3.4 Deployment of IEEE 802.1X in wireless LANs

IEEE 802.1X was designed to perform network access control on a port basis, i.e. on connection that has point-to-point characteristics. Some of these issues are discussed briefly as the following:

- A wired point-to-point connection has an implicit degree of security given by the nature of the connection itself and it happens namely on a cable or on a port, that is a means with well defined boundaries, where a certain degree of "work" is needed in order to eavesdrop the communication. A wireless connection, instead, does not have such features; consequently a communication can be easily eavesdropped by someone who has the right tools to do this.
- The use of individual MAC addresses in a wireless LAN, which is actually a shared medium network, allows its deployment in such environment. The IEEE 802.1X protocol exchange is anyhow not confidentiality-protected, nor are the EAP messages exchanged between the parties. This arises the necessity to use a secure association between supplicant and authenticator, in order to thwart eavesdropping and to enhance the communication at least with the degree of security that is proper to a normal wired point-to-point connection.
- The protection of the communication between the authenticator and the authentication server is an issue that is not within the scope of IEEE 802.1X, but is dependent on the protocol between them. If using a RADIUS server, a security association is supposed to exist between them, through the existence of a secret shared by them. Not the whole messages are protected however, but only the password or some other confidential information; integrity is guaranteed also. In order to protect the whole communication between authenticator and authentication server, it is advisable to transmit information on a secure association, for instance by using IPSEC.

4 EAP

The **Extensible Authentication Protocol (EAP)** [EAP] was designed to enhance the Point-to-Point Protocol (PPP) with additional authentication features. It is an extensible protocol, which means that it can always be enriched with new and stronger authentication mechanisms.

Although EAP was initially designed to be used on PPP connections, IEEE 802.1X uses it in order to exchange authentication information in a LAN environment. A typical EAP protocol exchange can be extracted from Figure 15.

The packet format is shown in Figure 17.

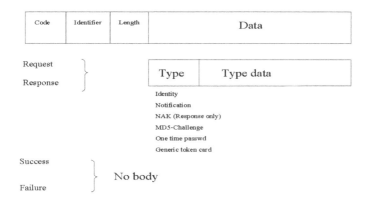

Figure 17: EAP packet format.

The *code field* includes information about the kind of packet, an *identifier* aids in matching requests and responses, a *length field* and a *data field*, who's content depends on the code field.

A packet can be a **Request**, a **Response**, a **Success** packet or a **Failure** packet. **Requests** and **responses** can be of different types, as specified in the Type field, which is given by the first byte of the data field.

An **Identity** packet is used as a request to ask for identification or as a response to state an entity's identity.

A **Notification** packet is used to convey a displayable message from the authenticator to the supplicant; it is intended to provide an acknowledgement of notification of some event.

The **NAK** packet is only used in response packets to indicate that the desirable authentication mechanism is unacceptable.

The other defined kinds of request or response packet specify authentication information depending on the mechanism being used.

A **Success** or **Failure** packet is sent to indicate the success or the failure of the authentication process and does not contain any body.

4.1 EAP-TLS

Transport Level Security (TLS) provides for mutual authentication and key exchange between two end points. EAP-TLS [EAPTLS] represents an extension to EAP: it defines further authentication mechanism, a protocol exchange in order to achieve authentication, security features negotiation, and a way to use it in an EAP compliant manner.

It can therefore be used within 802.1X since it doesn't require any modification to the current framework of the protocol. EAP-TLS is the result of the moving of the security protocol **TLS**, designed to be placed on top of a transport protocol, towards the link layer, within EAP to enhance it with additional features, thus not being obliged to design a complete new security suite.

TLS is a layered protocol and the protocol architecture is depicted in Figure 18. The **TLS Record Protocol** is the lower layer and it takes messages from the higher level protocols that need to be transmitted, fragments the data into manageable blocks, optionally compresses the data, applies a MAC, encrypts and transmits the result. The received data will be submitted to the reverting process. In order to achieve this, the TLS Record Protocols provide for a standard encapsulation of the data being passed from the higher levels.

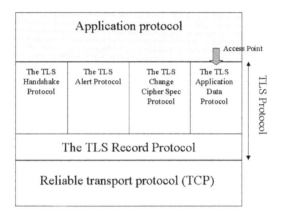

Figure 18: TLS Protocol architecture.

Every connection is characterized by a **Connection State**, which represents the operating environment of the TLS protocol. The connection state is made up of the security parameters, the compression state (the state of the current compression algorithm), the cipher state (the current state of the cipher algorithms), the MAC secrets and the sequence number (used to match different messages). At the beginning of the operations, there are no algorithms defined; this means that the current connection state does specify a NULL value for each of them. The TLS handshake protocol entities will proceed with a negotiation phase in order to set the values of the pending connection states. At the end of the operations the TLS change cipher spec protocol will send a message in order to fire the transition from the current state to the pending state. If any error occurs, the TLS alert protocol will send a message to handle them.

Once a connection state has been established, all the messages sent by the application level will be handled in order to be securely transmitted over the connection established by the TLS protocol.

EAP-TLS arises from the necessity to enhance EAP with additional features like mutual authentication, key exchange and cryptography parameters negotiation. TLS provides for such features but on top of a reliable transport protocol, like TCP.

The efforts spent for EAP-TLS has as a result the definition of a new EAP message type, the **EAP-TLS** message, in order to carry TLS messages on a link level protocol; the adaptation of the TLS protocol exchange to the EAP protocol exchange in order to make them compatible, and the definition of a fragmentation and a retransmission mechanism.

In order to allow a normal TLS protocol exchange in an EAP protocol exchange, and consequently in a 802.1X protocol exchange, every message sent from the TLS client (supplicant) to the TLS server (authentication server) is encapsulated in an EAP/Response/EAP-TLS message while the messages from the TLS server to the TLS client are sent in an EAP/Request/EAP-TLS message. There is one very important issue to note: the TLS conversation happens between the 802.1X supplicant (TLS client) and the 802.1X authentication server (TLS server). The 802.1X authenticator acts only as an entity needing the supplicant to authenticate itself but does not participate at all in the conversation and may even not understand what kind of messages it merely forwards.

Since the MTU of the link level may be less than the maximum size of a TLS message (2^{14} bytes), although it is not probable that a TLS message will be greater than a few kilobytes, it is necessary to define a fragmentation mechanism to face this problem; a very simple way to fragment EAP-TLS messages is provided by the protocol

A typical EAP-TLS protocol exchange is illustrated in Figure 19.

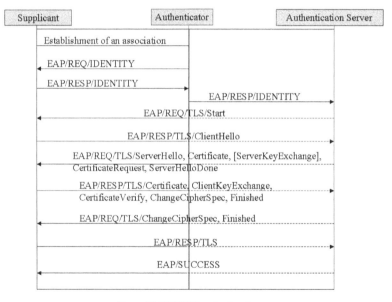

Figure 19: EAP-TLS protocol exchange.

As soon as an association has been established between the mobile terminal and the access point, the mobile terminal needs to be authenticated before allowing it to have access to the network. For this purpose the authenticator, i.e. the access point sends an EAP-Request/Identity to the supplicant, i.e. the mobile terminal. The supplicant will respond with an EAP-Response/Identity packet to the authenticator, which forwards the response to the authentication server.

The EAP server will then start the TLS negotiation phase by sending an **EAP-TLS/Start** packet to the EAP client and the conversation will proceed between what will typically be a RADIUS server, from now on called (according to the EAP-TLS definition) **EAP server** (authentication server), and the **EAP client** (supplicant). The authenticator will act as a pass-through server, forwarding and encapsulating EAP packets and is not required, to understand or being able to interpret the information, which it is dealing with. This will create some problems in designing a complete system based on 802.1X and EAP-TLS.

4.2 EAP-GSS and other extensions

EAP-GSS [EAPGSS] represents a further extension to the EAP protocol in order to make it support the different mechanisms that are available to those developers that use the Generic Security Service-Application Programming Interface, GSS-API [GSSAPI]. It is currently still at a draft level; therefore modifications of it should be expected in future releases.

The general concept behind it is exactly the same as the one behind EAP-TLS, i.e. to take a well-known negotiation protocol, in this case the Simple and Protected GSS-API Negotiation Mechanism (SPNEGO) [SPNEGO], and to place it into the framework of the EAP protocol. A new EAP type is defined for this purpose: the EAP-GSS type, which is assigned the value 14.

EAP-GSS provides for mutual authentication, cryptographic features negotiation and keys-exchange protocol, according to those mechanisms that are available to GSS-API programmers.

The negotiation is based upon the exchange of security tokens, which contain information about the available encryption and signing algorithms, or the parameters of a chosen algorithm. It needs a way to guarantee the reliable delivery of the messages that are sent during the negotiation as well as a fragmentation support. In order to have an effective network access control, it is even here necessary that the access point is kept informed of the outcome of the authentication exchange (as usual), of the key exchanged and of the mechanisms that have been negotiated between EAP-client and EAP-server. It is assumed that the EAP-server, i.e. the RADIUS server, will negotiate encryption algorithms that are supported by the access point.

As the saving of one round trip time may be significant, EAP-GSS tries to send the tokens containing the security parameters of the preferred authentication mechanism together with the negotiation token, sent at the beginning. If the EAP server will accept the client's preferred method, one round trip time is saved.

A basic protocol exchange can be seen in Figure 20. In its basic form, it appears actually to be more simple then EAP-TLS. The format of the message is nonetheless quite complex as well. The messages sent to negotiate the security features are integrity protected if the preferred mechanism supports integrity protection.

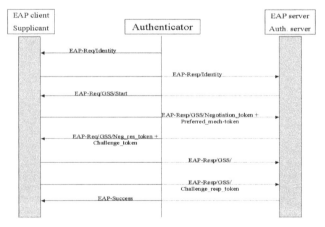

Figure 20: EAP-GSS protocol exchange.

The negotiation protocol allows furthermore to avoid completely the negotiation if the two communicating are willing to resume an old session with the previously defined security features. This is exactly what happens in EAP-TLS, which has the same feature; even in this case, this depends on the amount of time elapsed from the first or the last time that session was established or resumed.

5 Radius

The original aim of the **RADIUS** [RAD] was to develop a protocol that could carry authentication, authorization and configuration information between a **Network Access Server (NAS)** that desires to authenticate its links, and a shared authentication server. A typical environment is therefore made up of a network with many points of attachments (NAS), users that attach to the network through the NAS and willing to have access to the network, and a shared authentication server where information about the access features of the users can be retrieved.

5.1 Radius's general features

Radius defines a protocol for exchanging information between the NAS (RADIUS client) and an authentication server (RADIUS server) but it does not specify under which condition the authenticating peer, i.e. the entity wishing to access the network, should be granted access. Furthermore, it is not concerned with the communication between the NAS and the authenticating peer.

As hinted at in the previous paragraph, the RADIUS protocol is based on a client-server model: the NAS acts as a RADIUS client while the shared authentication server acts as a RADIUS server. It is also possible to have proxy RADIUS servers, which forward requests to other servers. The authentication of the communication between RADIUS server and the RADIUS client and the encryption of password sent over the network, are guaranteed by a shared secret, which is never transmitted over the network. The details are not specified in the standard and are implementation dependent; how the authentication key, i.e. the shared secret, is distributed depends on local policies.

One basic feature of the RADIUS standard is **extensibility**; it was designed in such a way that additional information, not specified in the first release of the standard, may be transmitted between client and server. This is achieved by defining attributes; each of them is characterized by an identifying code, a value and a length field, which allows to have values of different length for the same attribute type.

RADIUS works on top of UDP as a transport protocol for simplicity's sake. Indeed this simplifies the realization of the server but implies some issues concerning retransmission of sent packets, timing and storing of sent packets, before having received any response to them.

5.2 Basic operations

The RADIUS client is typically an access point to some network facilities, which wishes to know whether to grant access to one of its users, being connected to one of its point of attachments. The client's user submits information such as user name, password and possible services that it wishes to have access to. The RADIUS client sends a RADIUS **Access-Request** packet to the server, including the information submitted by the user. Passwords sent on the network are encrypted and all the packets are integrity protected by an **Authenticator** field included in the packet.

The RADIUS server receives the request and consults a database in order to retrieve information about the user: password, services, further requirements to authenticate the user, limitations or constraints for the user's access to the network are usually retrieved. If the information submitted in the first request are enough to grant access to the user, the server sends an **Access-Accept** packet; if there are conditions that make the server to deny access, it sends an **Access-Reject** packet. Otherwise it may happen that the server wants to challenge the client in order to verify further; in this case it sends an **Access-Challenge** packet, which the client has to reply to with an **Access-Request** packet containing the response of the challenge in the **Password** field.

If the server is not able to satisfy the request, it may forward it to another server, thus acting as a RADIUS client; by doing this it may add proxy information in order to deal correctly with the response to its request; such information should not be handled by other RADIUS entities.

It may also happen that a RADIUS server is temporarily unavailable; in this case, the NAS may submit the request to other RADIUS server, if it knows any.

5.3 RADIUS packets

An overview of the RADIUS packet format is illustrated in Figure 21.

Code	Identifier	Length
Authenticator		
Attributes		

Figure 21: RADIUS packet format.

The **Code** field specifies which kind of RADIUS packet is being sent; the **Identifier** field aids in matching requests to responds while the **Length** field indicates the length of the packet. The **Authenticator** field is used to provide authentication, while the **Attributes** contain information concerning the user of the client, which are necessary for the authentication process to succeed. Different kinds of RADIUS packet, identified by the Code field are the following:

- **Access-Request.** This packet is sent to a RADIUS server and includes information, which are used to determine if the client can be granted to have access to a specified NAS. It contains usually a user name, a password, service type, which is requested, the NAS identifier, and other attributes to better define the request.
- **Access-Accept.** It is sent by the RADIUS server to grant access to a user, after that authentication has successfully completed. It may contain information of the services, which the user can have access to.
- **Access-Reject.** Used to deny access to a user. It may contain a reason.
- **Access-Challenge.** This packet is sent by the server if it wishes to authenticate the client's user with a challenge. It usually includes a message to be displayed and a random number used as a challenge. The client has to reply to it, after the user has given a response, with a new Access-request packet.
- **Accounting-Request.**
- **Accounting-Response.** These kinds of packets are used if accounting options are active. They aim to collect information for user accounting in order to permit billing or statistical analysis. The usage and the attributes defined for RADIUS accounting are described in [RADAC] and [RADACT].

5.4 RADIUS attributes

This Section aims to give a brief and not exhaustive description of some RADIUS attributes, which are usually included in packet being sent between client and server. The major aim of them is to convey information that is necessary to authenticate users and to decide which types of service they may have access to. They have been designed in such a way to be completely extensible without modifying the basic protocol and often allow performing additional operations that were not considered at the beginning.

5.4.1 User related attributes

The most important attribute is probably the **User-Name**, which contains the name of the user, or more generally, the name of the entity willing to access the network; quite often it is accompanied with the **User-Password** attribute which indicates the password that the entity submitted to the client's system. It may also contain a response to a challenge issued by a server. This attribute is usually encrypted.

Other authentication schemes are also supported, such as CHAP; for this purpose, the **CHAP-Password** attribute can be included in the list.

5.4.2 NAS related attributes

In order for the server to retrieve the correct information form the database it needs to know which NAS the request came from (**NAS-Identifier**), its IP address (**NAS-IP-Address**), from which of its ports (**NAS-Port**), or of which type the port was (**NAS-Port-Type**). The NAS may grant the user a limited number of its ports (**Port-Limit**).

5.4.3 Service related attributes

Since the RADIUS server holds information about which services the user is allowed to have access to, or the user will request to have access only to a reduced set of available services, the **Service-Type** attribute included in the RADIUS packet. If included in a request packet, it should be considered as a hint or a request; if included in a response from a server it should be considered as a must. More instances of the same attribute type may be included in a packet. In case of a remote terminal service (login), it may specify which host to connect to (**Login-IP-Host**), which service to connect to (**Login-Service**), and which TCP port to connect to (**Login-TCP-Port**).

Other attributes specify information for callback services or LAT services. It is furthermore possible to specify messages to be displayed to the user, routing or addressing information and vendor-specific information (**Vendor-Specific**).

5.4.4 Session specific attributes

Certain services my be subject to time constraints, either as the maximum time to have access to the services (**Session-Timeout**), or as the maximum time to be allowed to stay in an idle state (**Idle-Timeout**). If a session terminates, it is possible to specify what action to take later (**Termination-Action***) or even a reason of the conclusion of a session

5.5 RADIUS EAP extensions

RADIUS was designed to be an extensible protocol; this means that it is possible to define new attributes in order to achieve new functions or to enhance and improve older ones. [RADEXT] defines new extensions which compensate for many missing features, among which the support for **Apple Remote Access Protocol (ARAP)**, support for EAP and other features which might be useful in order to increase the manageability of access control.

The EAP extensions represent a very important add-on in order to ease the integration of IEEE 802.1X and the RADIUS protocol. How and why this is possible is described in Section 8.6.

Since EAP allows many different authentication schemes, this flexibility is moved into the RADIUS protocol, thus improving further its already built-in extensibility feature. Through the use of EAP support a number of authentication schemes may be added, including smart cards, kerberos, public key, one time passwords, and others. This is achieved by adding two new attributes: **EAP-Message** and **Message-Authenticator**. How these new attributes used for EAP support with in RADIUS is described in the following sections:

5.5.1 EAP-Message

The EAP-Message allows to encapsulate a whole EAP message into a RADIUS packet, without modifying its structure or adapting the EAP message. The RADIUS server will then send the EAP message to some backend security server, which is likely to be placed on the same machine as the RADIUS server, as an additional module. They might communicate through some proprietary protocol.

It may happen that some RADIUS server does not understand the new attributes. In order to overcome that problem, and permit the packet to be proxied to another server, the NAS should copy the user name of an EAP-Response/Identity packet into the user-name attribute of the RADIUS packet. If the RADIUS server supports EAP extensions, it must respond with a RADIUS Access-Challenge packet containing an EAP-Message attribute with a valid EAP packet. If the NAS receives a RADIUS Access-Accept or an Access-

Reject packet, it must send an EAP-Success or an EAP-Failure packet to its user. If the RADIUS server does not support the EAP-Message attribute and no proxy operation is configured, the whole authentication process will fail.

The RADIUS client is responsible for retransmission of packets both to the user (the authenticating peer) and to the RADIUS server. [RADEXT] defines furthermore some facilities for fragmentation and reassembling, since it may happen that an EAP packet does not fit entirely in the attribute.

5.5.2 Message-Authenticator

The RADIUS messages are not integrity protected, but only authenticated. It is therefore necessary to provide the new extensions with integrity protection, in order to prevent any attacker to subvert the RADIUS/EAP communication and send messages never generated by one of the communicating entities. The Message-Authenticator attribute is used to protect all Access-Request, Access-Challenge, Access-Accept, and Access-Reject packets containing an EAP message, but may be used even to protect other authentication conversation. If this condition is not met or if the value of this attribute is different from the expected one, the authentication process fails.

The Message-Authenticator attribute is used to sign the RADIUS packets in which it is contained. It is an HMAC-MD5 checksum of the entire RADIUS packet, using the shared secret as the key. It is not needed when the User-Password attribute is present but it is used to prevent other kinds of attacks, such as "rogue server" attacks.

5.6 RADIUS and IEEE 802.1X

IEEE 802.1X defines a protocol exchange between an access point to some network and an entity that wants to have access to that network. RADIUS defines a protocol for allowing a Network Access Server (NAS) and a shared authentication server to communicate with each other. They can therefore work together for authenticating and performing access control on devices that attach to a network and want to use the services there available. This cooperation is further made easier since IEEE 802.1X defines an encapsulation for EAP packets and RADIUS has defined its own EAP extensions.

A complete and working integration would therefore be based on IEEE 802.1X for the communication between the wireless network access point and the mobile terminal and on RADIUS for the communication between the access point and the authentication server. The access point can in this way be very simple, since it simply has to encapsulate EAP packets in a RADIUS packet and forward them to the RADIUS server.

It may however happen that the RADIUS server does not support the EAP extension. In this case, the authenticator, for communicating successfully with the RADIUS server, should extract the information contained in the EAP packet and insert them into a RADIUS packet.

[RAD8021X] provides some more detailed description about how RADIUS can be integrated in a system that uses IEEE 802.1X, especially about the usage and the possible different meaning of the RADIUS attributes.

Part 2: Application of IEEE 802.1X in HIPERLAN 2

Part 2 illustrates the results that have been achieved while trying to solve the problem of integrating the IEEE 802.1X authentication standard and an HIPERLAN/2-based network:

- Chapter 6:   Deals with Analysis and Methodology aspects that have been considered while trying to solve the problem of integrating IEEE 802.1X and HIPERLAN/2.
- Chapter 7:   States about the IEEE 802.1X and HIPERLAN/2 from a protocol point of view.
  Chapter 8:   Describes the modifications in the HIPERLAN/2 need to be performed in order to integrate it with IEEE 802.1X
- Chapter 9:   How to deal with the Protocol exchange and authentication method.
- Chapter 10:   Describes the requirements that the IEEE 802.1X software module must meet in order to be housed and cooperate in the HIPERLAN2 network

6 Analysis methodology

This brief Chapter tries to roughly describe the aspects that have been considered while trying to solve the problem of integrating IEEE 802.1X and HIPERLAN/2, and why such aspects have been analyzed is roughly described in this Chapter.

Four basic issues have been considered in high detail:

* The protocols.
* The operation.
* The protocol exchange and authentication methods.
* The software requirements and architecture.

6.1 The protocols

The HIPERLAN/2 standard defines a very detailed protocol architecture. Each layer or sublayer carries out very specific tasks and defines an interface towards other sublayers within the HIPERLAN/2 standard or towards other protocols outside the standard.

IEEE 802.1X is a network access control standard, which is supposed to operate at the link level (layer 2 of the ISO/OSI protocol stack), but even to use its services (data transfer and indication of received data), thus putting itself above layer 2. Its position within the protocol stack is roughly the same as protocols like ARP or RARP, which belong formally to the link level but uses its services and whose Protocol Data Units (PDUs) are encapsulated in PDUs of link level protocols.

These considerations raises the necessity to understand how IEEE 802.1X can be inserted (if it can be inserted or rather put on top of it) in the HIPERLAN/2 protocol architecture and how it can collaborate with it. How this analysis was performed and the achieved results are described in Chapter 7.

6.2 The operation

A station, willing to communicate within a wireless network, has first to perform a set of operations in order to be allowed to send and receive data to other stations placed in the same radio cell or in other radio cells or even on other networks and subnetworks. The HIPERLAN/2 standard defines a procedure which is called *association* (look Chapter 2), which establishes a kind of link between the station and the access point to the wireless network. The association procedure is made up of different stages, including authentication; HIPERLAN/2 defines indeed its own authentication method.

It is necessary to decide how the operations included in the association procedure will work together with the operation defined in the IEEE 802.1X standard.

6.3 The protocol exchange and the authentication methods

IEEE 802.1x defines a protocol exchange between the different parts involved in the authentication operation. EAP encapsulated packets are sent between supplicant and authenticator, and between authenticator and authentication server.

It is therefore quite important to have a clear picture of what happens when authentication is performed and what the different possibilities are to perform such a task. Chapter 9 describes some of the possible protocol exchanges, and proposes a method to perform mutual authentication based on certificates, but without using the EAP-TLS extensions.

6.4 The software requirements

Since it is likely to have the IEEE 802.1X standard implemented in software, and part of the HIPERLAN/2 standard is implemented in software as well, it has been considered quite important to analyze the software aspects..

Chapter 10 depicts some possible software architectures and configuration for both the MT and the AP that could be used in order to integrate IEEE 802.1X and HIPERLAN/2

6.5 Why IEEE 802.1X and HIPERLAN/2

As pointed out in Chapter 2, HIPERLAN 2 defines its own authentication methods, which can actually be considered quite strong and reliable. However, there are some reasons that make it convenient to use IEEE 802.1X as authentication method and as a means to perform access control in a HIPERLAN/2-based network.

The main reason, on the engineering point of view, is that IEEE 802.1X allows the **centralization of the authentication function**. The authentication methods designed for HIPERLAN 2 require that the authentication function is performed in the AP. This implies that keys and/or certificates need to be stored in the AP or that those information need to be retrieved from some other site, and then be worked out. The computation happens anyway in the AP. This might be a problem in case of strong authentication methods, since the AP, handling many MTs, should be as smooth as possible. Furthermore, updating information would require to update all the APs installed in the network. By centralizing user information in another site than the AP, it would be furthermore possible to perform policy-based operation and make decisions based upon other criteria. The use of IEEE 802.1X in a HIPERLAN/2-based network allows to deal with user data in a centralized way, and to free the AP from tasks that may be computation-intensive.

Nowadays many companies claim that they are able to release products supporting IEEE 802.1X by the middle of the next year. The integration of this standard with HIPERLAN/2 would allow **compatibility** between different products. Furthermore it seems that the next release of the Windows operating system will support IEEE 802.1X as well; this would be quite important, since nowadays it is necessary to be compatible with the Windows OS.

EAP has been designed to be extensible: new authentication schemas could be added just by defining a protocol exchange and an EAP-type. Since IEEE 802.1X relies on EAP for performing authentication, the integration of IEEE 802.1X into HIPERLAN/2 would allow **extensibility** in the authentication of such a wireless network.

7 IEEE 802.1X and HIPERLAN/2: the protocols

This Chapter describes how IEEE 802.1X can be integrated from the point of view of the protocols, with the HIPERLAN/2 standard. It does not define any software architecture, but it carries out a study based only on the analysis of the official standards and documents.

7.1 IEEE 802.1X as a part of the HL/2 protocol architecture

HIPERLAN/2 defines different authentication protocols, based on pre-shared key or RSA private/public keys. The standard defines exactly which kinds of messages have to be sent for each authentication method, how long they are and how many. The MIB for HIPERLAN/2 defines five different authentication schemes:
- No authentication.
- Pre-shared-key authentication.
- RSA with 512-bits key.
- RSA with 768-bits key.
- RSA with 1024-bits key.
- Define a new MIB.

The HIPERLAN/2 protocol has been designed in such a way that management messages have always a known size. The DLC-PDU has a length of 53 bytes and each message fits in that size. If bigger, is transmitted above more than one DLC-PDU but even in this case, the total number of messages that need to be sent is known because the global size is known. The IEEE 802.1X packet has not a fixed size: the length of each message depends on the EAP type being used. The integration of the standards would result in a useless complication of the HIPERLAN/2 standard or in a reduction of the IEEE 802.1X standard, which would reduce its many useful features.

Furthermore, it may happen that a station, let's say a laptop computer, is endowed with many network connections, for instance a wireless LAN interface and an Ethernet interface, without performing routing or bridging tasks. Each of these network accesses might need to authenticate by using IEEE 802.1X, and each of them could use the same software module, thus saving development cost and resources on the machine. The conclusion is that it is useless and too complicate to place IEEE 802.1X into the HIPERLAN/2 protocol stack: it is better to let them separated in order to exploit them better. How this can be done is analyzed in the next Section.

7.2 Interaction between the HL/2 and IEEE 802.1X

This Section describes how the HL/2 protocol architecture can cooperate with IEEE 802.1X. In order to make it clear, the description goes through the steps that have been performed during the analysis.

7.2.1 First Step: basic assumptions

The packet format for IEEE 802.1X has not a fixed length while the HIPERLAN/2 DLC-PDU has a length of 53 bytes, 48.5 of them are exploitable to carry data. In order to allow IEEE 802.1x to send data across the wireless network, it is necessary to use or define a convergence layer, which performs the task of fragmenting and reassembling the packets, and of interfacing with the DLC sublayer. On the other hand, an encapsulation for EAP packets into Ethernet frames is defined and the HL/2 standard comprises what is called an Ethernet convergence layer. The conclusion is quite natural: using the HL/2 Ethernet convergence layer as a way to send EAPOL packets over the wireless network.

In the following discussion, the term "Ethernet" is mainly used as a synonym to the term "IEEE 802.3"; although this is formally not true, since the format of the packet is not the same, this has by now become a common habit. All the concepts used now on, are referred to the IEEE 802 architecture, including IEEE 802.3 and IEEE 802.2

7.2.2 Second step: interface to the protocols

The IEEE 802.1X standard defines the primitives it is going to use in order to send data across the network: they are DL_UNITDATA.request, to transmit a packet, and DL_UNITDATA.indication, to get an

indication when data is received. Such primitives require basically four parameters ([8023]): Source address, destination address, Service Data Unit (SDU), i.e. the packet to be sent, and the reception status.
On the other hand, the HL/2 Ethernet SSCS (Service Specific Convergence Sublayer) offers two primitives to the higher layers: DL_UNITDATA.request, to send data, and CL_UNITDATA.indication, to receive data. It appears that the primitives match quite good, but there are many aspects to be considered, by adapting a little bit the IEEE 802.1X implementation.
Second, but very important, is that the HL/2 Ethernet SSCS does not perform demultiplexing of packets. When the sublayer receives a packet , it does not interpret the length/type field, and is thus not able to pass the packet to the right protocol entity on the higher level. It simply takes the packet and passes it to some overlying Ethernet level. This situation is illustrated in Figure 22.

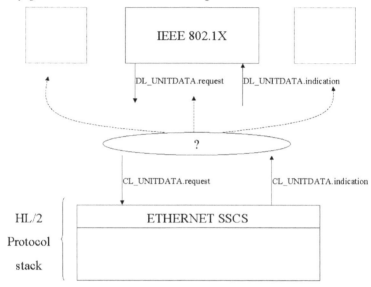

Figure 22: Primitives and demultiplexing

In order to solve this problem the best way is to use the **Logical Link Control (LLC)** sublayer, which is a part of the IEEE 802 standard, known as IEEE 802.2.

7.2.3 Third step: using LLC

The **Logical Link Control (LLC)** ([8022]), represents the upper sublayer of the link level, as defined in the IEEE 802 LAN architecture. Briefly, it defines different type of services and different primitives for each service; it performs demultiplexing of outgoing packets, and defines its own header to be appended to a SDU passed to its **Service Access Point (SAP)**. In order to be able to use the Ethernet type, as defined for the Ethernet type 2 standard (also known as D-I-X), it is convenient to use the **Sub Network Access Protocol (SNAP)** header, so not to rely on the LLC definition for the SAP addresses.
The LLC service type that seems to suit better to the needs of the IEEE 802.1X protocol, is the so-called Type 1 Service, which is an unacknowledged delivery of data. Services offered by the other operation types, like acknowledgment or connection-oriented delivery of data are not needed, because such services are available in HIPERLAN/2. Two basic primitives are available: DL_UNITDATA.request, and DL_UNITDATA.indication, which are actually the primitives needed by the IEEE 802.1X.

On the lower level, LLC requires basically three types of primitives: MA_UNITDATA.request, MA_UNITDATA.indication and MA_UNITDATA_STATUS.indication.

7.2.4 Fourth step: completing the model

The LLC is supposed to communicate with an IEEE 802 MAC sublayer; the HL/2 Ethernet SSCS expects as a SDU a packet, which is already complete. In a protocol view, provided in [HL2ETHSSCS], on top of the HL/2 Ethernet SSCS a level called **Ethernet/802.3 framing** is placed. The conclusion is that between the LLC sublayer and the HL/2 Ethernet SSCS, a kind of Reduced MAC level is needed, which performs the functions of creating the final packet to be passed to the underlying layer, adding and checking the length field, and matching the primitives of the underlying and overlying levels. The result is depicted in Figure 23.

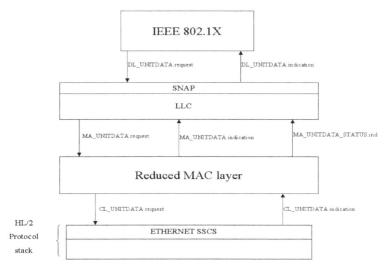

Figure 23: Protocol interaction between HL/2 and IEEE 802.1X.

The functions performed in the so-called Reduced MAC Layer can be extracted from [8023], where a detailed schema of the IEEE 802.3 MAC protocol functions is included. Figure 24 illustrates it.

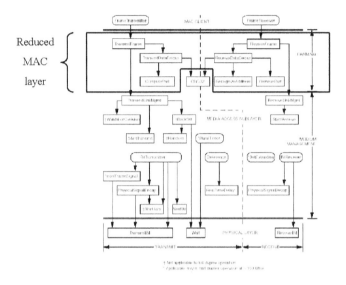

Figure 24: Reduced MAC layer (Source: [8023]).

7.2.5 Complete model

The complete model is that depicted in Figure 23. The IEEE 802.1X layer communicates with the LLC sublayer through its primitives, DL_UNITDATA.request and DL_UNITDATA.indication in order to send data or when it receives data. The reduced MAC level creates the complete Ethernet/IEEE 802.3 packet by adding the addresses, length and padding; this is then passed to the HL/2 Ethernet SSCS as a parameter of the CL_UNITDATA primitive.

When receiving a packet all heading information are removed by the layers that added them before, and the IEEE 802.1X packet is then passed to the right layer as it was sent by its peer. How the packets are affected by those steps is illustrated in Figure 25.

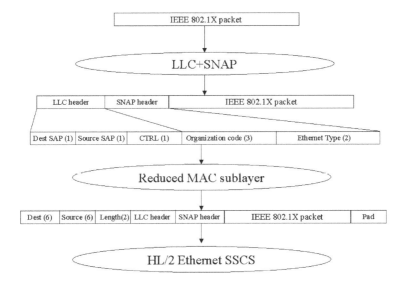

Figure 25: Flow of the IEEE 802.1X packet through the protocol stack

The model that has been so far presented represents how IEEE 802.1X can be integrated into HIPERLAN/2 from a *protocol point of view*. It does not consider any software issues or how such protocols are implemented in a complete working system. This means that this study is completely theoretical and only based on public and official standards.

8 IEEE 802.1X and HIPERLAN/2: the operation

This Chapter describes the modifications in the HIPERLAN/2 operation that need to be performed in order to integrate it with IEEE 802.1X. The basic aim was not to change any standard specification, but to adapt the operation in such a way to keep compliant with the standard.

The aspect of the standard that should be analyzed is the association procedure, since it decides what features need to be negotiated, including authentication, encryption and key exchange.

8.1 The association procedure

The association procedure carries out a set of operations, which will define the basic settings of the communications between the AP and the MT. During the association, the MT and the AP supporting IEEE 802.1X authentication negotiates that no authentication procedure will take place. On the other hand, they need to negotiate encryption and proceed with a key-exchange procedure. The AP and MT will therefore perform the following operations, within the normal association procedure:

- Negotiate for a suitable encryption algorithm.
- Negotiate for a suitable convergence layer, i.e. the Ethernet convergence layer.
- Perform a Diffie-Hellman key-exchange.
- Skip the native HL/2 authentication procedure.
- Complete the association.
- Start the IEEE 802.1X authentication
- If successful start the normal communication else disassociate.

Such behavior might be easily configured via management.

Furthermore, there is another issue about the key-exchange that needs to be briefly looked at. The Diffie-Hellman protocol, used by HL/2, is subject to a *man-in-the-middle* attack, since the keys are exchanged but no control is made over the identities of the partied being involved in the procedure. For this reason, HL/2 links the Diffie-Hellman public value into the authentication procedure. The key-procedure is actually only concluded when even authentication completed successfully. If the parties agree not to authenticate but to use encryption, and hence to exchange keys, they have to be aware that they cannot rely upon the identities of the parties. If authentication fails, the association has to be broken by disassociation and the result of the key-exchange has to be considered invalid. This aspect has to be considered in both the MT and the AP. It has to be noted anyway that the whole IEEE 802.1X exchange proceeds encrypted, so no other entity than the two involved in the authentication exchange can interpret the information being exchanged.

8.2 The controlled and uncontrolled port

One basic feature of IEEE 802.1X standard is the behavior of the point of attachment to the network, in which each point of attachment is split up into two ports, the *controlled port* and the *uncontrolled port*. Outgoing and incoming data are available on both the ports.

The controlled port is subject to the outcome of the authentication process. This means that data are allowed to flow through it only if the port is in the *authorized* state. The uncontrolled port allows the flow of data through it without any control. As the standard defines, IEEE 802.1X has the effect to model the point of attachment in a two-port system; this means that are not physically two ports, but the system has to simulate or reproduce the behavior of splitting up the access point to the network into two ports. This is actually one of the most important issues while integrating HIPERLAN/2 and IEEE 802.1X. In order to simulate this behavior, the possible management operations standardized by the HL/2 standard were analyzed first, and then, after realizing that it was not possible to act through management, another solution has been found out.

8.2.1 Management operations

In order to simulate the operations of the two ports, the management operations and available data were supposed to allow a quite deep control over the normal HIPERLAN/2 operations concerning the association procedure, the forwarding of packets and the prevention of such feature. More in detail, it was necessary to:

- To get complete information about the associations established at a certain time point (AP and MT).
- To be able to prevent packets to flow.
- To exert such a control in one or two directions.
- To exert such a control for different kind of packet.
- To know about disassociation, explicit or implicit.

8.2.2 Solution

The only feasible solution that allows implementing the mechanism of the double-port point of attachment is to act on the driver, since the HIPERLAN/2 standard does not indicate how this could be achieved.

There are two solutions, both of them consisting in modifying in the driver the behavior that is done for every single packet that it is received. The solutions are different from each other, depending on how the data are treated in the driver, whether on an association-basis or a global basis. In the first case, the solution is actually easier than in the second case.

8.2.2.1 A single thread for each association

If a single thread deals with only one association, then the behavior that the driver should observe is:

```
for each incoming packet inc_packet{
        if (status!=authorized)
            if(packet_type(inc_packet)!=allowed)
                    block_packet();
}
 for each outgoing packet out_packet{
        if(status!=authorized)
            if(OperControlledPortDirections==Both)
                    if(packet_type(out_packet)!=allowed)
                        block_packet();
}
```

In this piece of pseudocode, inc_packet is the incoming packet, out_packet is the outgoing packet, *status* indicates the state of the variable, *packet_type()* is a function that return the value *allowed* or *not-allowed* depending if the type of packet is supposed is flow even if the port in unauthorized state, *block_packet()* is the function that performs the blocking function.

8.2.2.2 One process for all associations

If only one single-threaded process deals with all the association, then the behavior of the network interface driver is given by the following piece of code:

```
for each incoming packet inc_packet{
        ID = get_source_mac_id(inc_packet);
        if (status(ID) != authorized)
            if(packet_type(inc_packet)!=allowed)
                    block_packet();
}
 for each outgoing packet {
        ID = get_dest_mac_id(out_packet);
        if(status(ID)!=authorized)
                if(OperControlledPortDirections(ID)==Both)
                    if(packet_type(out_packet)!=allowed)
                        block_packet();
}
```

In this case it is necessary to extract the MAC ID of the source of the packet (get_source_mac_id()) for incoming packets the destination MAC ID (get_dest_mac_id()) for outgoing packets and then check the status for the port corresponding to that association.

9 IEEE 802.1X and HIPERLAN/2: protocol exchange and authentication methods

IEEE 802.1X makes use of EAP in order to perform authentication. This allows deploying several authentication schemes, which are available. So far, there are four standardized EAP methods, namely MD5, General Token Card, One-Time Password and EAP-TLS. MD5 is equivalent to the PPP Challenge Handshake Authentication Protocol (CHAP) ([CHAP], [MD5]), General Token Cards and One-Time Password are not further explained in [EAP], while EAP-TLS is described in [EAPTLS]. A further method is described in [EAPGSS] but it is still at a draft level.

More methods might be added in order to meet particular conditions or requirements, or for keeping update with new authentication technologies. In the case of wireless LANs (HIPERLAN/2 in this case), it can be interesting to notice how strong the participation of the authenticator is in each different authentication schema, since it will be the AP to play this role and it is usually supposed to be as small and simple as possible.

At the beginning, basic issues about the authentication process and a brief survey of different authentication exchanges is provided, without focusing on a particular authentication mechanism, but underlying different degree of participation of the involved entities.

9.1 Authentication methods: basic issues

This Section depicts some basic issues about the authentication methods that should be used in a system based on IEEE 802.1X and HIPERLAN/2.

9.1.1 Challenge-response

All the authentication mechanisms deployed in a wireless network should be based on a challenge-response protocol, since this avoids the sending of passwords in clear, or even encrypted, on the network. The issue is to send a challenge, which is a randomly generated number to the supplicant. The supplicant replies by sending the challenge back encrypted or digested with some key-based digest algorithm. It can even send it back together with the challenge in clear. Such methods are indeed based first on strong random-number generation function and second, on an algorithm for which it is impossible (or at least very difficult) to work out the key having an encrypted piece of data and the clear text.

The algorithms that can be used are MD5 (see [EAP], [MD5], [CHAP]), HMAC-MD5 ([MD5], [HMACMD5]), RSA if using some public-key cryptography for authenticating. A token card-based system follows the same rules.

What happens (after identities have been exchanged) is:

1. The Authenticator A sends a challenge C to the supplicant S.
2. S replies by sending a response R to A, where $R=Enc(C, k)$. Enc () is the encryption function, and k is a key. Such a key is algorithm dependent. It might be a shared symmetric key or a private key.
3. A sends the authentication outcome to S, which may be success or failure.

This example has considered only what happens between supplicant and authenticator, while the intervention of an authentication server has been neglected.

9.1.2 Mutual authentication

In a corporation environment, the possibility to authenticate the network access point to the device willing to attach to the network might not be so important, because of two reasons. First, the possibility to perform a rogue-server attack is quite low, since the physical environment of a corporation is usually quite protected. Second, a corporation network is supposed to have only one network provider; it is quite difficult to have corporation environments with a provider different from the normal one. This issue is not very different in a wireless network. Though the coverage of such a network might "go outside" the normal protected physical environment, placing a rogue access point outside the corporation environment might not be difficult because of the propagation conditions of a wireless network. An HIPERLAN/2 MT establishes an association with the AP with the strongest signal. A rogue AP, placed outside a building, should transmit with a very high power to overcome the difficult propagation conditions of a corporate building.

A public environment, or more generally an environment where public network access in available, is instead quite easy to make "untrusted". First, it would not be too difficult to create a faked access point; with a wireless network, such operation is even easier. Second, such an environment could offer network connection by many network operators. MT willing to establish a connection, could not base only the network id, but should require authentication of the AP, in order to be sure.

In case of mutual authentication, the operations are the following:

1. A sends a challenge C_1 to S.
2. S responds with R_1=Enc$_1$ (k_1, C_1) and sends a new challenge C_2.
3. If S authenticated successfully, A responds with R_2=Enc$_2$ (k_2, C_2), otherwise sends an error message.
4. If A authenticates successfully, S sends an OK message.
5. A terminates the authentication conversation.

Enc$_1$ () and Enc$_2$ (), like k_1 and k_2 might be the same algorithms or have the same values, or might be different. These are environment-independent features.

The actual communication happens between supplicant and authentication server, hence the mutual authentication occurs between those two entities. However, this feature can be neglected by considering the authenticator and the authentication server belonging to the same system. What happens, if observed from the supplicant point of view, is that it authenticates the entity on the "other side". It actually does not perceive the presence of authenticator and authentication server, who might also be placed on the same physical system. This feature is illustrated in Figure 26.

Since the native HIPERLAN/2 authentication mechanisms perform a mutual authentication, it is reasonable to conclude that IEEE 802.1X deployed in a HL/2-based network should use an EAP method that implements mutual authentication as well.

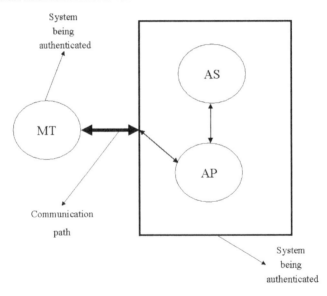

Figure 26: Mutual authentication.

9.2 Basic authentication schemas

Before the very first authentication, two entities being involved in the authentication process, meet, physically or virtually, in order to exchange two authentication keys, to get a certificate, to receive a token card or to register biometrics data. After the *first contact*, the normal authentication can proceed normally. The authentication schema will always be based on a challenge-response mechanism, but no details about the algorithms are provided here, since it does not change the protocol type. Mutual authentication has not been considered either, though it would involve adding only one or to messages in the communication, usually containing a further challenge and a further response.

9.2.1 Strong participation of the authenticator.

An example of authentication exchange involving a strong participation of the authenticator will here be illustrated. The authenticator is in charge of sending an EAP-Request/Identity and an EAP-Request/OTP (or some other EAP type) to the supplicant. The Authentication server is only in charge of authenticating and authorizing the supplicant, but is not strongly involved in the protocol exchange. An example is given in Figure 27. In this situation, the RADIUS server receives an Access-request packet, with the response given as a password, and the challenge included as well. The RADIUS server will elaborate the challenge and the response and check in its database for authorization.

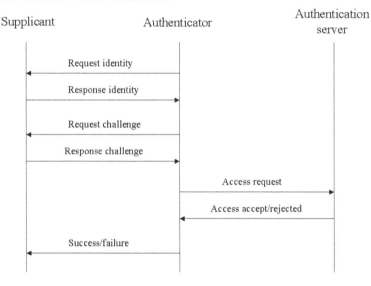

Figure 27: Authentication schema with strong participation of the authenticator.

9.2.2 Less participation of the authenticator

In this case, the challenge is sent by the AS, forwarded by the authenticator. The response is sent by the supplicant and forwarded to the authentication server by the authenticator. It is assumed that the RADIUS server does not support the EAP extensions. This means that the authenticator has to extract information from the EAP packet and create a new RADIUS packet. An example is given in Figure 28.

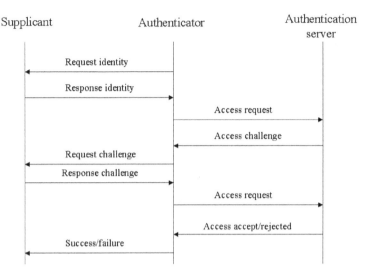

Figure 28: A different authentication schema.

9.2.3 Minimal participation of the authenticator

This authentication schema is characterized by the authentication server performing all the important actions that concern with the authentication process. If the exchange of a key is comprised in the EAP method, then the authenticator has obviously to deal with it, but it should be avoided to have the authenticator to generate a key. For instance, using EAP-TLS, a key is shared by supplicant and authentication server; such a key has been generated by those entities, which are both *TLS-aware*. In order to let the authenticator know the key, this key could be transferred to it by the supplicant, using the EAOPL-Key message or by the RADIUS authentication server, by including it in some attribute, mainly vendor-specific attributes. Actually, the Microsoft vendor-specific attributes consider an attribute to exchange a key between the NAS and the authentication server.

Such a schema looks more or less like the one illustrated in Figure 28, with the exception that all the messages forwarded from the authenticator to authentication server are actually included in the EAP-message attribute of a RADIUS message.

IEEE 802.1X was designed as an authentication standard and as a means to perform access control; furthermore, the use of certain EAP types, may give the possibility to generate a key to be used for encryption. Such a key might be exchanged within the EAP conversation or with the EAPOL-key message.

9.3 Authentication exchange

To use HIPERLAN/2 or some other kind of network does actually not make any difference in the protocol exchange. This example makes use of the EAP method defined as "MD5" in [EAP], which is actually equivalent to PPP-CHAP [CHAP]. The messages that are sent to the RADIUS server are EAP messages encapsulated in a RADIUS message.

The assumptions that are made are the following:

- An association has been established between the MT and the AP. The MT acts as a supplicant while the AP acts as authenticator. The authentication server is placed on a network reachable by the AP, but it is not placed on the same system.
- Encryption is active: a pair of Diffie-Hellman has been exchanged and all the messages are exchanged in an encrypted form.
- Authentication has not been performed during the association procedure.
- Packets are not allowed to be sent by the supplicant and, if the OperControlledPortDirections parameter is set to Both, are not allowed to reach the supplicant either.
- The IEEE 802.1X layer is triggered to start operations.

The operations and the protocol exchange that are performed by the parties are described in detail; to indicate a message from the MT to the AP, the following notation is used: MT->AP; a packet from the AP to the authentication server is indicated as follows: AP->AS, and so on.

1. MT->AP:
   EAPOL-Start packet.
2. AP->MT:
   EAPOL-EAP packet encapsulating an **EAP-Request/Identity** packet.
3. MT->AP:
   EAPOL-EAP packet encapsulating an **EAP-Response/Identity** packet; the identity is expressed in some format understandable within the network.
4. AP->AS:
   RADIUS packet of type **Access-Request**. The following attributes are included: *User-Name*, attributes about the NAS (*MAC-address*, etc), *EAP-message* (which contains the EAP packet sent by the supplicant), *Message-authenticator*.
   The AS (Radius server) looks in its database, likely an Active Directory, for the user being authenticated. A challenge is generated and sends back in the next step.
5. AS->AP:
   Radius packet of type **Access-Challenge**, containing the following attributes: *User-name*, attributes about the NAS, *EAP-message*, *Message-authenticator*; the challenge might be included in the *Reply-message* attribute as well.
6. AP->MT:
   EAPOL-EAP packet encapsulating an **EAP-Request/MD5** packet. This is exactly the same EAP packet encapsulated in the RADIUS packet sent previously from the AS to the AP. The EAP-Request/MD5 packet contains the challenge.
7. MT->AP:
   EAPOL-EAP packet encapsulating an **EAP-Response/MD5** packet. Contains the response to the previously sent challenge.
8. AP->AS:
   RADIUS packet of type **Access-Request**. The following attributes are included: *User-Name*, attributes about the NAS (*MAC-address*, etc), *EAP-message* (the one received from the MT), *Message-authenticator*. The response sent by the MT is also included in the *Password* field.
   The RADIUS server elaborates the received response and checks for authorization in the Active Directory.
9. AS->AP:
   RADIUS packet of type **Access-Accept** or of type **Access-Reject**, according to the outcome of the authentication process and the authorization check. An EAP packet containing the result of the authentication is also included in the RADIUS message. It might be **EAP-Success** or **EAP-Failure**. Note that the authentication can be successful but the authorization might be denied, according to some local policy, bound to that user. Configuration information might be included as well in some attributes
10. AP->MT:
    EAPOL-EAP packet encapsulating an **EAP-Success** or **EAP-Failure**, depending on the authentication outcome. Furthermore, the *Authorization Result Code* field of the packet is set to *authorized* or to *unauthorized*, according to the outcome of the RADIUS server.

9.4 A certificate-based authentication method: a modest proposal

9.4.1 The protocol exchange

Only the communication path between supplicant and authenticator will be considered; it assumes that the actual flow happens between supplicant and authentication server, where the authenticator acts as a pass-through server, and the EAP messages to the authentication server are encapsulated in RADIUS packets. Basically what happens, after that identities information has been exchanged, is:

1. The authenticator A sends an **EAPOL-EAP** packet, encapsulating an **EAP-Request/New_method** packet, containing a challenge C_1 to the supplicant S.

2. The supplicant S sends an **EAPOL-EAP** packet, encapsulating an **EAP-Response/New_method**, containing a response R_1 to the challenge C_1 ($R_1=Enc\ (Pr_S\ ,C_1)$, where Pr_S is the supplicant's private key), a new challenge C_2, and, if needed, a certificate or a link to a certificate stored somewhere.

3. If the response sent by the S was correct, A replies with an **EAPOL-EAP** packet, encapsulating an **EAP-Request/New_method**, containing a response to the new challenge (with $R_2=Enc\ (Pr_A\ ,C_2)$, where Pr_A is the authenticator's private key), and if needed a certificate or a link to a certificate stored somewhere. If the response sent by the authenticator was not correct, an **EAP-Failure** packet is encapsulated in the EAPOL-EAP packet.

4. The supplicant acknowledges the authenticator, and gives an indication of the result of the authenticator's authentication.

5. If the authentication was successful on both part and if there is no reason to deny access to the supplicant, the authenticator sends and **EAPOL-EAP** packet, encapsulating an **EAP-Success** packet, otherwise and **EAP-Failure** packet.

9.4.2 The format of the EAP packet

In order to allow the previous protocol exchange, the packet format must allow to send different kinds of data according to different situation.

The format here discussed is the one of the **EAP-Request/New_method** or **EAP-Response/New_method**, and is illustrated in Figure 29. The first byte is a control byte and the fields have to be interpreted in the following way:

CH: Indicates if the packet contains a challenge

RE: Indicates if the packet contains a response to a challenge previously sent.

REF: Indicates if the packet contains a reference to a certificate stored somewhere.

CE: Indicates if the packet contains a certificate.

SU: Indicates if the received response was successful. Sent by the supplicant or by the authenticator.

FA: Indicates if the received response was not successful. Sent by the supplicant.

The other fields may contain a challenge, a response, a reference to a certificate stored somewhere or a certificate. The order is the same as indicated in the picture. If one of the fields is indicated as not present in the control field, then it is missing. There will never be misinterpretations in the position of the fields.

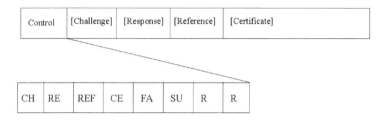

Figure 29: Packet format of new method.

9.4.3 Issues

Many issues need to be discussed about this proposal, and will be discussed in the following sub sections:

- Link is not reachable.
- No network connection.
- The format of the packet.
- Certificate management and policy.
- Authentication server for the supplicant.

9.4.3.1 Link not reachable

It may anyway happen that a link is unreachable due to networks problem or because the referenced certificate has been deleted. Since it is not possible to distinguish between different situations, in such a situation the best solution seems to consider authentication unsuccessful and not to authenticate the user. In certain situations, let's say in closed network where the link references a certificate with local validity, if it is possible to distinguish between reasons why the link is unreachable, a user might be successfully authenticated and authorized. In this situation, reauthentication may occur with a shorter timeout.

9.4.3.2 No network connection

It may actually happen that it is not possible to reach a link to a certificate because a network connection has not been granted yet.

What can happen is that the reference to the certificate is unreachable or that a CRL cannot be obtained for that certificate; in this situation, the supplicant should acknowledge the authenticator and check the credentials as soon as possible, i.e. when network access is available. The supplicant can try to verify the authenticator's credentials basing upon some certificate that has been retrieved previously, and checking later for CRLs. A complete verification has to be done anyway before considering the process concluded and proceeding to the normal transmission stage.

9.4.3.3 Format of the fields of the packet

As previously hinted at, a link to a certificate might have global validity or local validity within a network; it may be expressed as URL or as an index in some local database. Furthermore, the format of the challenge and of the response might depend on how strong the encryption algorithm is requested to be; the certificate might be compliant with [X509] or [PKCS6]. It turns out that the format of the single fields must be discussed further and in detail. One first suggestion could be to add a *version* field, in order to distinguish between different formats.

9.4.3.4 Management and policy

Dealing with certificates implies a set of basic issues that so far has not been solved; such issues imply storing certificates, how to deal with CRLs, the validity scope of such certificates, and so on. The general solution is to come to a local assessment in order to deal with such problems and to be able to use certificates, even if in a reduced scope.

9.4.3.5 Authentication server for the supplicant
In the case of mutual authentication, even if the authenticator leads the authentication conversation between the two parts, the authenticator is being authenticated also by the supplicant. One issue is: "Do the supplicant need an authentication server in order to authenticate the authenticator?"
In order not to complicate the situation it can be accepted that the supplicant authenticates the authenticator on its own; this choice may be justified by the fact that only authentication is needed, while authorization, access control or accounting are not needed.

10 The software requirements and architecture

This Chapter aims to describe the requirements that the IEEE 802.1X software module must meet in order to be housed and cooperate in an HIPERLAN2 network, and to illustrate some possible architectures for both MT and AP.

10.1 General issues

Since the best choice appeared to integrate IEEE 802.1X externally, it is now necessary to figure out what kinds of software requirements need to be meet and some possible architecture.

The actors being involved are basically four: the *HIPERLAN/2 network interface driver*, the *IEEE 802.1X module*, *modules corresponding to higher levels* and a *control or interface module*.

The interactions between the different modules are as follows. After a new association has been established, the control module still prevents the transmission of other packets than management or authentication, and starts the authentication operation by triggering the IEEE 802.1X module. After it has concluded, according to its outcome, the control module will either allow the transmission or disassociate. During the operation, some kinds of protocols (SNMP, AFS…) are allowed to flow, regardless of the authentication outcome. The control module, besides interfacing the other modules and keeping control over the operation, might perform other tasks such as buffering or delaying of data. The basic interactions are depicted in Figure 30.

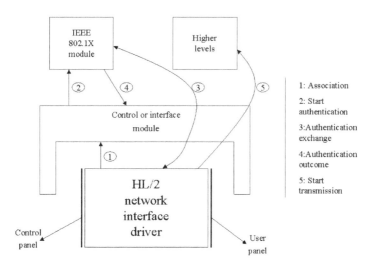

Figure 30: Basic software architecture and interactions

An important issue that needs to be analyzed is regarding <u>disassociation</u>, which has not been considered in the previous model. It may happen implicitly, in case of the loose of radio connection, or explicitly, if, for instance, the user logs off. In case of implicit disassociation, this may happen if an **MT_ALIVE** procedure terminates with concluding that the MT is not there any more. The interval, which establishes the frequency of such procedure, called **mt_alive_interval**, which can be set by management operation, should be decided with regard to security policies.

Another important aspect to consider regards reauthentication: when the reauthentication timer expires and the authentication procedure is performed again, if the outcome is negative, the control model should be informed, in order to allow it to prevent further transmission. It has anyway to be pointed out that, since the transmission should be encrypted, it is quite easy to perform an open-session attack.

10.2 Software architecture on the MT-side

In this case, the accuracy on the AP must be much greater, because it is responsible to enforce authorization, and, more generally, to grant a secure access to the network to authorized devices.

In an MT where more than one interface is available, the IEEE 802.1X should be designed in such a way to be interface-independent. What should happen is that such a module is triggered each time an interface gets up; this means that a new instantiation is created for each of them, as soon as that interfaces transits in the *active* state. As soon as the process is over, the module might be deactivated or kept active in order to keep a state of the active connection, which is anyway not requested. A basic architecture is depicted in Figure 31. The different interfaces are kept under control by an *Interface controller*. As soon as an interface starts to be active, it triggers (T) the *interface supervisor*, which is interface dependent. The interface supervisor (S) supervises the interfaces and starts the IEEE 802.1X module as soon as the startup processes have completed. The interface controller is started at boot-time. The network supervisor keeps on checking all the time in order to track changes in the network interface and act properly on the IEEE 802.1X module. Furthermore, if the user logs off, then the IEEE 802.1X module has to send an EAPOL-Logoff message.

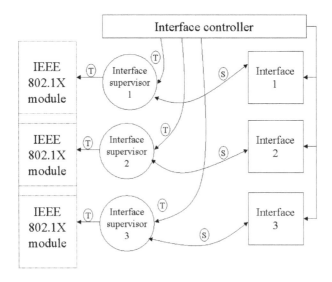

Figure 31: Basic software architecture.

After an association has been established, the IEEE 802.1X module, triggered at the right time, starts the authentication process by sending an EAPOL–Start packet, according to the behavior of the state machine, which expresses how the protocol should act. The point here is: How to know that an association has been established and how to trigger the IEEE 802.1X module? There are basically two possibilities:

- Keep the control module spinning on some variables in the HL/2 network interface driver, likely the management variables that are in charge of storing the information about active associations.
- Let the network interface driver trigger the control module that will further trigger the authentication module in order to start

Before authentication has been successfully concluded, data are not supposed to be sent, since they might to be lost because not accepted by the AP. What can happen is that data to be sent might be buffered before being sent if authentication has not been concluded yet, be non-acknowledged, forcing higher levels to try again later or simply discarded.

Another interesting issue is what happens with DHCP: it can be completely ignored, trusting in its own retransmission features, or be triggered after successful authentication. In the first case the DHCP timer will expire the first time, maybe a second time but then, when authentication has completed, it will get a reply. In the second case, the DHCP client will send a request and get a reply as soon as network connection is working.

According to what has been depicted in this Section, there can be two different software architectures for the MT, which will be illustrated in the next two Subsections.

10.2.1 A simple software architecture for the MT

The basic feature of this model is given by its straightforwardness: it defines a reduces set of interaction with the network interface driver, in order to ease the implementation and portability and no communication with higher levels. Packets are allowed to be sent without any hindrances; if authentication has not concluded yet or has concluded unsuccessfully, it is up the higher levels to realize that there is no network connection.

There are two interactions with the HL/2 driver. The first one happens when <u>association</u> occurs: the IEEE 802.1X module is activated in order to deal with the authentication exchange, by the interface supervisor, if present, or by the driver itself. In order to perform this, it is necessary to change one part of the HL/2 network driver, called the *association manager*. As soon as association is established, it has to send a signal to the interface supervisor in order to start authentication.

The other kind of interaction happens at the end: if <u>disassociation</u> occurs, an EAPOL-Logoff packet should be sent. This might be not so important, because it is mainly the AP that has to deal with this problem. It would anyway be advisable to trigger the IEEE 802.1X module to send a notification of the disassociation to the AP, or when the user starts the logoff procedure.

A particular situation happens when mutual authentication is active, because in this case the MT should not send packets when the authenticator does not manage to authenticate successfully.

This basic architecture is illustrated in Figure 31.

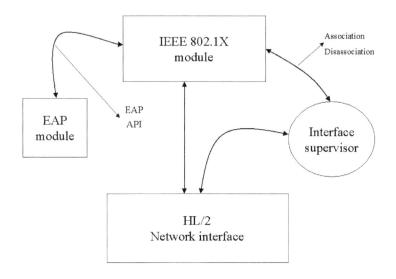

Figure 31: A simple architecture for an MT

The figure illustrates also the relationship with the EAP module given by EAP APIs, which allow using the services that are made available by the different EAP methods.

10.2.2 A complete architecture for the MT

This model is characterized by more complex interactions between the different part, which made up a system based on IEEE 802.1X authentication and authorization. The interface supervisor is much bigger and exerts a stronger control over the network interface driver; furthermore, it talks with the higher levels as well. It keeps track as usual of new associations and disassociations but it also prevents packets to be sent if authentication has not successfully completed; this feature might be very useful in case of mutual authentication. If a higher layer wants to send data across the network but authentication or authorization has not been completed yet, than the packets can be buffered until the network connection is perfectly working; the higher layers do not note the difference. On the other hand, if authorization is denied, the data that need to be sent can be non-acknowledged. In this way the system is more efficient but the implementation of such a model is much more difficult and implies much more investigation. An example is given in Figure 32.

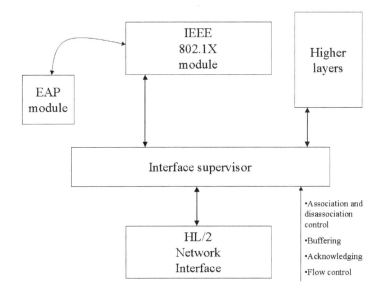

Figure 32: A complex architecture for the MT.

10.3 Software architecture on the AP-side

On the side of the AP, the software requirements are much higher because it is up to the AP to enforce authentication and access control and thus to prevent unauthorized devices to access the network and the services there available. The AP represents the first point of attachment and thus the first "check-point". In order to let things work, it is necessary to exert a quite strong control over the AP operation, which are not feasible through normal management operations, as seen in Chapter 8. How such control is exerted depends on how the AP is actually implemented; this Section tries anyhow to point out some common issues and to design a possible software architecture.

Basically the operations that should be performed are the following:

- An MT asks the AP to establish an association; the negotiation occurs as illustrated in Chapter 8: negotiate encryption and Ethernet SSCS, perform exchange of keys.
- When the HL/2 association successfully completed, the AP should not consider the whole procedure as done, i.e. the MT is not allowed yet to access the network. This means that the AP does not forward packets coming from that MT, and sends to the MT only if the OperControlledPortDirections parameter is set to In. Packets that are not forwarded are discarded, except the ones that are allowed by some internal policy, like authentication. Furthermore, the MIB is not updated yet.
- The IEEE 802.1X module starts and performs authentication triggered by a control module, which is necessary even in the AP, unless it has been opportunely modified. During the whole procedure, the AP keeps on not allowing the MT to transmit.
- If the MT is authorized to access the network, the AP proceeds with the normal operation, otherwise a disassociation procedure is started.

- During a session, the reauthentication keeps counting and as soon it expires, a new authentication procedure starts; if it concludes unsuccessfully, the MT is disassociated, otherwise the session is kept alive.
- Events like a received EAPOL-Logoff packet, an unsuccessful MT-Alive procedure, or a disassociation for some reasons should be tracked.

It has to be noticed that the authorization status and the session timer should be kept alive for each association, i.e. for each associated MAC-Id during the whole session. This means that in a situation of maximum load, the AP has to keep track of up to 256 association, which is the maximum number of associations allowed for each AP.

An example of possible architecture is depicted in Figure 33.

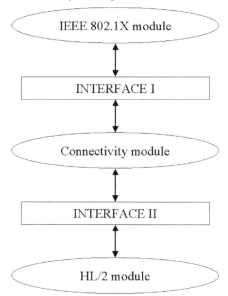

Figure 33: Basic architecture for an AP.

In this example, the IEEE 802.1X module communicates with a so-called *connectivity module*, whose aim is to allow communication with the HL/2 module. The connectivity module can be considered divided into two parts, one part which is dependant on how the IEEE 802.1X module has been defined, and one part which is dependent on how the HL/2 has been designed.

Interface I defines how the connectivity module communicates with the IEEE 802.1X: it is given by a set of signals between the two modules (creation of a new association, disassociation, outcome of the authentication and authorization process) and a set of parameters for each signal (result of the authorization process or the reauthentication process, MAC id, etc).

Information for each association might be stored in the AP, in the connectivity module or in the IEEE 802.1X module. Since the IEEE 802.1X defines a set of variables and timers for each port, i.e. for each association, it seems reasonable to keep there much of the information. Other information might be kept in the connectivity module, hence avoiding to complicate too much the HL/2 module.

Interface II performs the task to put the HL/2 module in communication with the connectivity module, i.e. to look for new association and disassociation, and to watch for correct forwarding of packets.

It has to be noticed that even though the IEEE 802.1X module is unique within an AP system, it has to deal with many associations. This means that a kind of multithreading architecture is needed, since many associations may happen at the same time. It is up to the AP's implementation how such a system is dealt with, if to associate more than one MT at the same time in a concurrent way or to serialize them. A possible architecture for the AP is given in Figure 34.

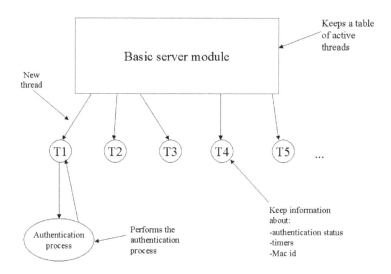

Figure 34: IEEE 802.1X architecture in the AP.

The *basic server module* waits to be triggered or to receive some event by the connectivity module, which has been previously defined. If a new association is started, this module launches a new thread that will deal with the new association. A table of all current threads is kept in the basic server module.
Each thread keeps information about the authentication status, the timers, the MAC-Id of the current association. When required, a new thread is started to perform the authentication process; the result is then stored in the launching thread. The authentication thread might finish when the procedure has concluded or kept active, stuck in one of the states of the state machine, which is there implemented.

Part 3: Implementation and testing

This part depicts the basic features of the implementation that has been achieved. The basic aim of the implementation was not to produce a commercial version of the software, but to demonstrate and test the issues defined in the previous Chapter.

- Chapter 11: Depicts the basic issues of the implementation that has been carried out in order to demonstrate what has been discussed and analyzed in the previous part Implementation
- Chapter 12: The testing methodology and results are illustrated as well.

11 The implementation

The actual implementation is slightly different, the software architectures that have been described for a number of reasons. Since there are no HIPERLAN/2 products available yet, it is impossible to test the prototype with such a network. For this reason the packets are sent on a normal Ethernet network. Also the prototype does not really interact with the network interface: the authentication process does not start when the interface goes up but a specific function of the prototype is called. On the AP side, this is even more evident, since an AP was not available. Furthermore, the interface towards EAP is not complete, but it supports only a set of basic functions. More details are given in Appendix B.

11.1 Basic features of the prototype

The prototype includes two basic parts, the supplicant and the authenticator. Both parts, which are more or less correspondent to the "IEEE 802.1X modules" introduced in chapter 10, have been implemented as normal Windows-style Dynamic Link Libraries, have a multithreaded structure.

The authenticator includes a RADIUS client in order to make use of an external authentication server for performing the actual authentication function. The normal WINDOWS 2000 RADIUS server has been used, which is included in the Internet Access Service (IAS), on eof the services made available in the WINDOWS 2000 Server edition.

The different software architectures there presented, included always a sort of intermediate module, called supervisor module or connectivity module, aiming to act as an interface between the IEEE 802.1X and the network interface drivers. In the implementation such a module has not been carried out, for a number of reasons due to the time to design and implement it was not enough and the aim of the thesis work was not to implement a commercial prototype but something that could prove the basic features of IEEE 802.1X.

There was not the possibility to use a working HIPERLAN/2 network, since products are so far not available yet. In order to let the prototype working, and to avoid to use the WINSOCK 2 interface, a sort of *intermediate driver* has been used. Such a driver, used as a normal Windows-based Dynamic Link Library (DLL), gives the possibility to send Ethernet packet on the network, without being obliged to cross the complete protocol stack. This driver has been made available by the Software Development group, working at Ericsson Enterprise.

The prototype has been implemented in C/C++. The functions that are needed by different classes or by the main part of the prototype have not been encapsulated in a class implementation. On the other hand, the functionality of the state machines used in the standard, and the functions used by them, have been encapsulated in a class. So there is a class for each state machine, and they are instantiated in the main file.

The different parts of the prototype have both been implemented as DLLs, such binding them to the Windows operating system. The prototype makes thus use of the WINAPI 32 for implementing multithreading, namely the functions that allow to run a new thread, to synchronize access to shared variables, to read in the register, to load a DLL or to make use of a COM object.

Each part of the prototype is dived in several files. Functions that are used by both modules and that have access to global variables are grouped in the same file, while the functions that don't make use of global symbols are included in a different file; the implementation of each class is given in separate files. Furthermore, three different header files are used to define symbols used by both parts or by only one part. The following files are included in both modules:

- 802_1Xv9.h. Contains the basic definitions for the IEEE 802.1X, version 9, standard
- timer.cpp. Contains the implementation of the timer class functionality.
- generalFunc.cpp. Contains the implementation of some functions that are needed across the various files and that don't make use of the global symbols defined for those systems, i.e. either the supplicant system or the authenticator system.
- globalFunc.cpp. Contains the implementation of functions that are needed across the files and that make use of global symbols. Its implementation changes a little bit between the supplicant's and authenticator's system.
- Keyreceive.cpp. Contains the implementation of the *Key Receive* state machine, which is needed in both the supplicant's system and the authenticator's system.

The following files are included only in the supplicant's system:

- supplicant.h: Contains definitions of symbols and classes only needed in the supplicant's system
- supplicant.cpp: Contains the implementation of the supplicant class.
- Maindll.cpp: Contains the functions exported by the IEEE 802.1X module implemented on the supplicant's system.
- eapFunction.cpp. Contains functions needed to interface with the EAP API on the supplicant's system.
- supp_key_tran.cpp. Contains the implementation of the *Supplicant Key Transmit* state machine.

The following files are included in the authenticator module:

- Authenticator.h: Contains definitions and global symbols only needed in the authenticator's system.
- Maindll.cpp. Contains functions exported by the IEEE 802.1X module implemented on the authenticator's system
- authenticator.cpp. Contains the implementation of the authenticator class.
- AuthKeytrans.cpp. Contains the implementation of the *Authenticator Key Transmit* state machine.
- Backend.cpp. Contains the implementation of the *Backend Authentication* state machine.
- ContrDir.cpp. Contains the implementation of the *Controlled Directions* state machine.
- Reauthen.cpp. Contains the implementation of the *Reauthentication* state machine.

11.2 The MT-side implementation

The implementation on the side of the MT looks basically like in Figure 35. The main DLL module instantiates the objects corresponding to the different states machines and allocates the memory which is shared with other functions and the various objects. The common memory area contains buffers that are needed to transmit frames over the network, variables for the support of multithreading, variables for allowing the different functions to communicate and those symbols declared global in the IEEE 802.1X standard.

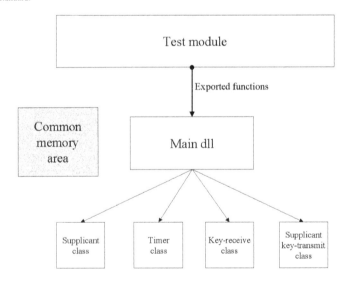

Figure 35: The MT-side implementation

All the functions and the class declarations are reported in Appendix B.

The window 2000 OS supports EAP and in order to make use of EAP, the EAP APIs made available by Microsoft have been used. However, such APIs are quite complex depending on the EAP method that has been chosen. For A detailed description about how the EAP APIs have to be used is provided in Appendix C.

11.3 The AP-side implementation

The implementation of the IEEE 802.1X module on the AP side is basically similar to that on the MT-side, as Figure 36 depicts. The Main DLL module, as in the MT, is responsible for allocating resources, exporting functions and instantiating the objects needed on the side of the authenticator's system.

Although the authenticator's system is not supposed to run on a Windows platform but on some kind of embedded real time operating system, it has been implemented using the system calls typical of Windows system, since it had to be tested on such a platform. As a consequence it has been implemented as a DLL, even though this was not necessary.

Even in this case the software needs some adjustment, not done during the work for a lack of time. Its architecture should be increased, management features should be added as well as the counters that keep track of the state of the system and its behavior. The exact description of the files that make up the authenticator's system is given in Appendix B.

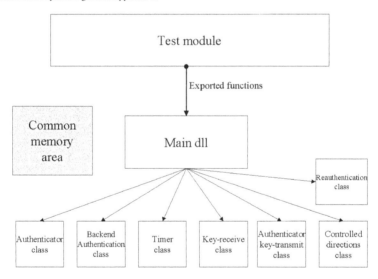

Figure 36: The AP-side implementation.

In order to enforce authentication and obtain authorization information acts as a RADIUS client sending RADIUS messages that obtain the EAP packet received from the supplicant. The client which was provided by the company VIRCOM Inc., is a COM/Active X object that after have been installed on the system can be easily be used with in the code. The EAP extensions is also adapted by the company developers and the work become easier. After having instantiated an object and obtained a reference to the Idispatch interface, it is necessary to open a request by providing the information about the user being authenticated and the RADIUS server.

12 Testing

Since the availability of time and hardware resources were limited, certain features have not been tried out. The basic aim was to accomplish an elementary conversation between the authenticator **Port Access Entity (PAE)**, the supplicant PAE and the Authentication server, in order to understand how IEEE 802.1X behaves and interacts within the environment that has been presented in Chapter 1.

12.1 The testbed

This Section describes the environment used for testing the implementation, from both the hardware and the point of view of the software.
The system to be tested was made up of the following components:

- The supplicant's system.
- The authenticator's system.
- The authentication server.
- The users' database.

The components are shown in Figure 37, together with their interactions.

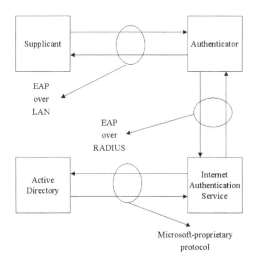

Figure 37: The components of the testbed.

The **supplicant's system** represents the entity to be authenticated; in an environment as described in Section 1.4 it would be a mobile terminal requiring access to a network based on HIPERLAN/2. The supplicant PAE, i.e. the part of the system dealing with the IEEE 802.1X protocol was completely implemented from scratch, except EAP, which was provided by the Microsoft APIs. The system was running on a Windows 2000 Server platform.
The **authenticator's system** represents the entity enforcing authentication and controlling the status of the point of attachment to the network. In a HIPERLAN/2-based network it would be the access point. The authenticator's system includes a RADIUS client supporting the EAP extensions; such client was provided

by Vircom Inc, a Canadian software company. Even this system was running on a platform based on the Windows 2000 operating system.

The **authentication server** was given by the **Internet Authentication Service (IAS)**, which is a part of the Windows 2000 Server operating system. It is a RADIUS compliant authentication server that supports the EAP extensions. It is able to authenticate using either a local stored database or an **Active Directory** placed somewhere in the Windows 2000 domain. The testing was based looking up for the users in an Active Directory.

The **users' database** was an Active Directory that stored the users of the system, their passwords and their dial-in properties. The Radius server was configures to connect to it and enforce authentication of the users. Since there was a lack of hardware equipment, all the components were placed on only two PCs, as showed in Figure 38. Furthermore, the network that connected all the different components were not a wireless LAN but a simple Ethernet based network.

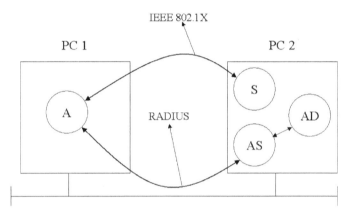

A: Authenticator

S: Supplicant

AS: Authentication server

AD: Active Directory

Figure 38: The used testbed.

12.2 The testing methodology and results

Since the amount of available time was quite limited, the choice has been to start testing the most important parts in order to get the system to work. Basically, what has been tested were the communication paths between the main parts of the system, and roughly the behavior of the state machines.

12.2.1 The RADIUS communication

The first communication path to be tested was the RADIUS conversation between the authenticator and the authentication server. In order to ease this task and limit the scope of the operation, a brief test program was written, containing the setup operation of the RADIUS client, the opening of a new RADIUS request, the adding of an EAP-message attribute to the request and the transmission of the request. At the beginning a normal password-based method was used, to be sure that the RADIUS client and server were able to communicate and that the RADIUS server was able to look up the user in the Active Directory. Afterwards, the scope was broadened to an authentication method based on EAP, first a simple EAP type based on the transmission of a password in the EAP message (sample EAP method made available by Microsoft) and then EAP-MD5; EAP-TLS was not tried out. The problem was basically to understand what kind of attributes the RADIUS server expected in the first message, if an EAP-Request/Identity had to be included or not. The answer was given by a carefully read of the related RFC and by trial, of course.

It turned out that it was necessary to include the RADIUS *User-name* attribute in each request sent to the RADIUS client. The first request sent to the server was an Access-Request message, containing the name of the user, some information about the RADIUS client (NAS-IP, NAS-identifier, NAS-port) and the service required, namely *Authenticate-only*. Furthermore, it was necessary to include the EAP-Response/Identity packet sent by the supplicant.

According to [RADEXT] it may happen that the NAS does not know the identity of the authenticate (as called by that RFC) and does not even send an EAP-Request/Identity packet to the supplicant. In this situation the NAS server sends a request to the RADIUS server containing no user name and an empty EAP-message attribute inside. This approach frees the authenticator from sending the EAP-Request/Identity message, which is instead sent by the RADIUS server and included in a Access-Challenge message. This approach has been tried out also but it did not work since the Windows 2000 IAS server does not support this feature. If guest-access was not allowed and EAP was set up as the authentication protocol, it was necessary to include the user name attribute, which had to be copied by the authenticator from the EAP packet into the RADIUS message, and an EAP-message attribute. In this situation the RADIUS server replies with a Access-Challenge message, containing an EAP-message attribute. By using MD5 as EAP type, the server replied with an EAP packet of type MD5 containing a challenge.

12.2.2 Communication between supplicant and authenticator

The other communication path to be tested was between the authenticator and the supplicant. This was much more troublesome since the packet had to be sent over the Ethernet medium without crossing the TCP/IP protocol stack. In order to achieve this, a test program was written as well as in the former case, in order to isolate the functions related to the transmission of packets and perform a more effective troubleshooting operation.

The solution was given by a so called *Ethernet Gate*, a DLL provided by the Software Development group; the Ethernet Gate was able to communicate directly with the network interface driver, and was installed on the system as an additional network protocol. It allowed to send packet by calling a simple function, and to receive packets by registering a receiving function to the DLL. Such function, being part of the authenticator's and supplicant's systems, was called by the Ethernet Gate each time a packet was received; it had then to deal with the packet.

The main problem was to append the MAC destination and source addresses to the packet, since the software that dealt with the transmission of the packets, used that information to send the packet and did not accept the addresses as parameters.

Another problem that was met by testing the Ethernet Gate was to deal with the different conventions of representing strings of bytes, i.e. *big endian or little endian*. It turned out that some data types used throughout the system used different conventions than required, obliging to change many of the data types or by adjusting them by hand each time.

After having tested the communication path, the results and corrected code was then applied to the supplicant's and the authenticator's systems.

12.2.3 Testing of the state machines

As described in Chapter 11, both the supplicant's system and the authenticator's system have been developed as normal DLL exporting a set of functions to be called by the module dealing with the interface to the network driver. Since such a module was not implemented, a test program has been written, that simulates the call sequence that is expected from the interface module. Such a test program loads the DLL, and calls the functions exported by the DLL.

After having tried out the communication between supplicant and authenticator, and between RADIUS client (authenticator) and RADIUS server (authentication server), the state machines have been tested using the test program, described previously. Such a test program made first a call to the *setup()* function, contained in both systems. This allowed to test out if the allocation of the needed resources was successfully. After that the function *start()* was called to observe the behavior of the state machines, that were thus activated as threads, and at the end a call to the function *stop()* allowed to debug deallocation of resources and shutting down of the systems. Other features were not tried out due to a lack of time.

12.2.4 Testing results: summary

As already pointed out, the testing session has been carried out in a quite limited amount of time, which obliged to neglect many features and to focus on some basic issues that have been considered more interesting, such as the communication between the RADIUS client and the RADIUS server, since the RADIUS extensions for EAP are relatively new. Furthermore such feature represents a very important issue in the whole system, because it allows to centralize authentication and authorization and to free the access point from this task, which might be quite resource demanding.

On the other end it was very useful to look at the IEEE 802.1X protocol exchange between supplicant and authenticator, and how the packets received by the authenticator from the supplicant and the authentication server, were forwarded to the other part of the authentication exchange.

At the end of the testing phase, which actually represents only the early stage of a complete testing session, the result was a working system with basic features, able to authenticate a user, i.e. the supplicant, through the authenticator, by the authentication server. The used EAP method was EAP-MD5, a simple challenge-response based authentication scheme that allowed nonetheless to appreciate the potentialities of a complete commercial release.

Part 4: Conclusions and final remarks

This part contains the conclusions that have been drawn during the thesis work and how and what can be done further to complete and continue this work. In particular, there are certain aspects of the analysis that need to be further analyzed, the implementation needs to be refined and the testing activity needs to be concluded. Furthermore, this part includes references, bibliography and some appendixes that deepen certain aspects of the thesis.

- Chapter 13: points out the achieved result and the conclusion later provides some guidelines to continue this thesis work

13 Conclusions and final remarks

13.1 Summary

This master thesis aimed to analyze the IEEE 802.1X standard and to study the possibility to integrate it with the standard for wireless networks known as HIPERLAN/2.

Part 1 of this report describes the main features of the IEEE 802.1X and of the HIPERLAN/2 standards; furthermore, it provides an overview of other protocols and standards that may collaborate with IEEE 802.1X in enhancing with data-security a wireless network. More emphasis was laid upon those features that were then further analyzed in this report, like security in HIPERLAN/2, the deployment of IEEE 802.1X in shared-media networks, the attacks that might be countered by using Port Based Network Access Control in a network with a high number of point of attachments, and the protocol exchange that occurs between the different parts of a system based on this standard.

Part 2 shows in a quite detailed way how IEEE 802.1X could be deployed within an HIPERLAN/2-based network. It analyzes what happens with the protocols, proposing a solution for their interaction; it goes through the operations that occur during the setup phase of HIPERLAN/2 and illustrates how they should be adapted and modified. Furthermore, it looks inside the authentication protocols and schemes that might be deployed and which of them fits better into a wireless network; a new certificate-based authentication method is also proposed. Eventually a number of possible software architectures are depicted, which would allow the usage of IEEE 802.1X in a system based on HIPERLAN/2.

Part 3 outlines the features of the implementation that has been achieved and how it has been tested. It has been shown that the software architecture used within the system is not very far from the ones being depicted in chapter 10 and that it could be easily adapted to one of them. In the case of the authenticator's system a bigger work should be performed, to adapt to the operating system adopted on an access point, likely a real time embedded operating system, with support for multithreading.

13.2 Achieved results

The first part of this report, apart providing a technical overview of the different topics that were necessary to carry out the work, has underlined some issues that were further deepened later on. It has pointed out that it is necessary to pay some attention while deploying IEEE 802.1X in a wireless network, because authentication information exchanged on a shared-medium LAN without being encrypted can easily be snooped and used for some kind of attacks. On the other hand HIPERLAN/2 already includes its own security features, which arose the questions whether it is really useful to enhance it further; the answer has been provided in part two.

The discussion about EAP, and especially about EAP-TLS has underlined some issues of such an authentication method, that make believe that its adoption within a wireless network is not the best solution; Chapter 9 has suggested a simple authentication method that could be used as an alternative.

Part 2 analyzes in detail some aspects of the integration of HIPERLAN/2 and IEEE 802.1X. In particular it suggests a solution on how to interface the protocol stack of HIPERLAN/2 and assigns a place to IEEE 802.1X within it, by defining how they should communicate. It has been seen that it is necessary to lay down some constraints in the association procedure of HIPERLAN/2, in order to allow a different kind of authentication to take place instead of its native one, and that some changes should be performed in the software performing the network functionary to be able to implement the behavior of the controlled and uncontrolled ports on the AP side.

In the analysis of the different protocol exchanges and authentication method, it has been underlined that because of the nature of the AP, usually a poor-endowed piece of hardware with small computational power and memory, with a relatively smart operating system, the impact on it should be as small as possible. As a consequence it is advisable to delegate much of the operations to the authentication server, which can be arbitrarily powerful and scalable. Furthermore, the moving of authentication and authorization out from the access point, allows for a more scalable solution in terms of number of users, access control policy, adoption of certificate-based authentication methods, redundancy and hence reliability. In order to underline the extensibility and flexibility of EAP, and as a consequence of IEEE 802.X, a new simple certificate-based authentication method has been proposed, which provides only for authentication.

Another aspect that has been faced up concerned a possible software architecture to be implemented in the AP and the MT. It turned out that the software adjustments to be done in the MT can also be very simple, delegating to higher levels the task to deal with absence of any network connection. On the AP side instead, which is in charge of enforcing access control to the network, it is instead necessary to design a very accurate architecture to avoid any possibility to elude Port Based Network Access Control.

Part three, by describing the achieved implementation and explaining the test methodology, has underlined some of the aspects that have already been pointed out in Part two. It has seen which aspects of the whole system are particularly important and interesting, which aspects need to be analyzed further and in great detail, and what needs to be developed further.

To conclude, this master thesis has demonstrated that it is possible to deploy IEEE 802.1X in a network that allows wireless access using HIPERLAN/2. It is shown how this can be achieved, which modifications should be applied to the systems and how a possible complete environment could look like. This last point has been confirmed by the implementation that has been carried.

13.3 Future work

The task to study and analyze a standard like IEEE 802.1X, to propose a way to integrate it in a wireless protocol and to implement a prototype to prove the statements made previously, is actually quite ambitious and with a lot of aspects to consider and many points of view to keep in mind. Considering that a master thesis has to be concluded in a limited and reduced amount of time, the natural consequence is that many points are neglected or analyzed quite roughly.

Starting from the last point, namely the implementation, as already pointed out in Chapter 11, what has been carried out needs to be revised and improved. First it needs to be adapted to the modern software engineering concepts, then its design needs to be made smarter, and less resource consuming. Eventually it needs to be tested in a complete and exhaustive manner.

Concerning the analysis of how Port Based Network Access Control can be deployed in HIPERLAN/2, there are at least three aspects that could be deepened. First, a device accessing a wireless network using HIPERLAN/2 is likely to be a *mobile* or a *portable* device; furthermore, such a network will probably have more than one access point, allowing the mobile terminal to associate with different access points. In this scenario, it would be quite interesting how IEEE 802.1X could behave or need to be adapted when a **handover** from one cell to another happens.

Second, Chapter 4 has introduced **EAP-TLS**, as a means of enriching EAP with more sophisticated features, such as security features negotiation, exchange of encryption keys, and certificate-based authentication. How EAP-TLS would adapt to the HIPERLAN/2 security studies could be an area of big interest.

Third, the Windows 2000 operating system has a support for the **Kerberos** authentication method, which will probably be used as the main authentication scheme. Both EAP and RADIUS are able to support Kerberos: EAP can be easily adapted to it, while there are already IETF Drafts documents ([RADKER]) proposing RADIUS extensions for allowing the usage of Kerberos within it. How Kerberos, IEEE 802.1X, HIPERLAN/2 could fit together can be an interesting subject to analyze in detail.

Broadening the scope of this discussion, there are two other aspects about Port Based Network Access Control that can be considered for a possible future work. The same discussion that has been faced up in this thesis can be done for **IEEE 802.11**: how this wireless network standard would benefit from endowing it with IEEE 802.1X and in which way this can be achieved, can be considered the subject for another master thesis project.

On the other hand, only the corporation environment has been considered has a deployment area. **Public environments** are likely going to have their breakthrough in the next years, but examples of working public are already available. The security issues are quite different in this kind of environment and how IEEE 802.1X can affect and improve the security of such networks is another very interesting matter.

References

[8021X9]   IEEE Draft P802.1X/D9, "Standards for Local and Metropolitan Area Networks: Port based Network Access Control", November 2000.

[HL2OV]   ETSI TR 101 683, V1.1.1, "Broadband Radio Access Networks (BRAN); HIPERLAN Type 2; System Overview", February 2000.

[HL2PHY]   ETSI TS 101 475, V1.1.1, "Broadband Radio Access Networks (BRAN); HIPERLAN Type 2; Physical (PHY) layer", April 2000.

[HL2DLC]   ETSI TS 101 761-1, V1.1.1, "Broadband Radio Access Networks (BRAN); HIPERLAN Type 2; Data Link Control (DLC) Layer; Part 1: Basic Data Transport Functions", April 2000.

[HL2RLC]   ETSI TS 101 761-2, V1.1.1, "Broadband Radio Access Networks (BRAN); HIPERLAN Type 2; Data Link Control (DLC) layer; Part 2: Radio Link Control (RLC) sublayer", April 2000.

[HL2MAN]   ETSI TS 101 762, V1.1.1, "Broadband Radio Access Networks (BRAN); HIPERLAN Type 2; Network Management", October 2000.

[HL2PBCL]   ETSI TS 101 493-1, V1.1.1, "Broadband Radio Access Networks (BRAN); HIPERLAN Type 2; Packet based Convergence Layer; Part 1: Common Part", April 2000.

[HL2ETSSCS]   ETSI TS 101 493-2, V1.1.1, "Broadband Radio Access Networks (BRAN); HIPERLAN Type 2; Packet based Convergence Layer; Part 2; Ethernet Service Specific Convergence Sublayer (SSCS)", April 2000.

[HL2BUE]   ETSI TS 101 761-3, V1.1.1, "Broadband Radio Access Networks (BRAN); HIPERLAN Type 2; Data Link Control (DLC) Layer; Part 3: Profile for Business Environment", September 2000.

[80211]   IEEE Std. 802.11,1997 Edition, "IEEE Standard for Wireless LAN Medium Access Control (MAC) and Physical Layer (PHY) specifications".

[8023]   IEEE Std 802.3, 1998 Edition, "Information technology - Telecommunications and Information exchange between systems - Local and metropolitan area networks - Specific requirements - Part 3: Carrier sense multiple access with collision detection (CSMA/CD) access method and physical layer specifications".

[8022]   IEEE Std 802.2, 1998 Edition, "Information technology - Telecommunications and information exchange between systems - Local and metropolitan area networks - Specific requirements - Part 2: Logical Link Control".

[MD5]   IETF RFC 1321, "The MD5 Message-Digest Algorithm", R. Rivest, April 1992.

[CHAP]   IETF RFC 1994, "PPP Challenge Handshake Authentication Protocol", W. Simpson, August 1996.

[HMAC]   IETF RFC 2194, "HMAC", H. Krawczyk, M. Bellare, R. Canetti, February 1997.

[HMACMD5]   IETF RFC 2085, "HMAC-MD5 IP authentication with Replay Prevention", M Oehler, R. Glenn, February 1997.

[OTP]   IETF RFC 2289, "A One-Time Password System", N. Haller, C. Metz, P. Nesser, M. Straw, February 1998.

[X509]   CCITT Recommendation X.509, "The Directory - Authentication Framework", 1988.

[PKCS6]   RSA Technical Note, "PKCS #6: Extended-Certificate Syntax Standard, version 1.5", November 1, 1993.

[EAP]   IETF RFC 2284, "PPP Extensible Authentication Protocol (EAP)", L. Blunk, J. Vollbrecht, March 1998.

[TLS]   IETF RFC 2246, "The TLS Protocol Version 1.0", T. Dierks, C. Allen, January 1999.

[EAPTLS]   IETF RFC 2716, "PPP EAP TLS Authentication Protocol", B. Aboba, D. Simon, October 1999.

[EAPGSS]   IETF Draft < draft-aboba-pppext-eapgss-02.txt>, "EAP GSS Authentication Protocol", B. Aboba, 21 November 2000.

[SPNEGO]   IETF RFC 2478, "The Simple and Protected GSS-API Negotiation Mechanism", E. Baize, D. Pinkas, December 1998.

[GSSAPI]   IETF RFC 2743, "Generic Security Service Application Program Interface Version 2, Update 1", J. Lynn, January 2000.

[RAD]   IETF RFC 2865, "Remote Authentication Dial In User Service (RADIUS)", C. Rigney, S. Willens, A. Rubens, W. Simpson, June 2000.

[RADEXT]   IETF RFC 2869, "RADIUS Extensions", C. Rigney, W. Willats, P. Calhoun, June 2000.

[RADAC]   IETF RFC 2866, "RADIUS Accounting", C. Rigney, June 2000.

[RADACT]   IETF RFC 2867, "RADIUS Accounting Modifications for Tunnel Protocol Support", G. Zorn, B. Aboba, D. Mitton, June 2000.

[RAD8021X]   IETF Internet Draft <draft-congdon-radius-8021x-02.txt>, "IEEE 802.1X RADIUS Usage Guidelines", Paul Congdon, Bernard Aboba, Tim Moore, Aswhin Palekar, Andrew Smith, Glen Zorn, Dave Halasz, Andrea Li, Albert P. Young, John Roese, July 2000.

[RADKER]   IETF Internet Draft <draft-kaushik-radius-sec-ext-05.txt >, "Radius Security Extensions using Kerberos v5", Kaushik Narayan, August 2000.

Tables of figures

Bibliography

"HiperLAN/2 – The Broadband Radio Transmission Technology Operating in the 5 Ghz Frequency Band", Version 1.0, Martin Johnsson, HiperLAN/2 Global Forum, 1999.

"HIPERLAN type 2 for broadband wireless communication", Jamshid Khun-Jush, Göran Malmgren, Peter Schramm, Johan Torsner, Ericsson Review No.2, 2000.

"Internet Security: Firewalls and beyond", Rolf Oppliger, Communications of the ACM, May 1997/Vol 40. No. 5.

"Security in Computing, ", Charles P. Pfleeger, Second Edition, Prentice-Hall International, Inc, 1997. ISBN: 0-13-185794-0.

"Windows 2000 Security Technical Overview", White Paper, Microsoft Corporation, 2000. www.microsoft.com/windows2000

"Active Directory Architecture", White Paper, Microsoft Corporation, 2000. www.microsoft.com/windows2000

"Internet Authentication Server for Windows 2000", White Paper, Microsoft Corporation, June 9,2000. www.microsoft.com/TechNet/win2000/ias.asp?a=printable

"Secure networking using Windows 2000 Distributed Security Services", White Paper, Microsoft Corporation, 2000. www.microsoft.com/windows2000

"Securing Windows 2000 network resources", Scenario Guide, Microsoft Corporation, 2000.

"Benefits of Wireless Networks", Jim Geier, 15 August 2000. www.wireless-nets.com/whitepaper_wireless_benefits.htm

"State of the Wireless LAN Industry", Mack Sullivan 1998. http://www.wlana.com/learn/stateind.htm

"Security white paper", 2000. http://www.wlana.com/learn/security.htm

"Ethernet", Marc Smith, http://www-ee.eng.hawaii.edu/~msmith/XCoNET/Ethernet.htm

"Wireless wonders Coming your way", Peter Rysavy, Network Magazine, May 1, 2000. http://www.networkmagazine.com/article/NMG20000510S0024

"The wireless market: growth hinges on the right solution", White Paper, Ricky Gradwohl, Tsantes & Associates, Prepared for Radiata, Inc.

Appendix A: The authentication process

The authentication process involves different entities: the *Claimant*, whose identity needs to be verified and ensured; the *Principal*, i.e. the entity the claimant states to be and that has a set of rights and privileges; and the *Authenticator*, i.e. the entity that requires and enforces authentication. The authentication function might however involve another entity, i.e. the system that actually performs the verification. If authentication concludes successfully, than the claimant turns out to be the principal and can therefore perform the operation for which it has the rights and privileges. In the IEEE 802.1X standard, claimant and principal are called the *Supplicant*, while the authentication function is performed by the *Authentication Server*.

Authentication, i.e. the process of verifying the claimant's identity, can be based on three basic paradigms:

- Something you know.
- Something you have.
- Something you are.

The first paradigm, i.e. something you know, implies that the claimant knows a password or a key that the principal is supposed to know. The second one implies the possession of a token card or a smart card that only the principal can have; the third one corresponds to some biometrics method, like checking fingerprints or retina pattern.

All three paradigms share a basic aspect: all three imply the knowledge of something not by **one** entity but by at least **two** entities: the entity performing authentication needs to know that the principal *knows*, *has* or *is* something. This implies one very important issue: before the first authentication, the principal and the authenticating entity meet to establish this common knowledge; a *first contact* is needed to decide on which basis an authentication should occur. Furthermore, this contact has to happen in an absolute safe way.

The certification of a public key should happen in such a way also. If the entity being certified is an email address, then the certification can happen remotely, through the e-mail itself, assuming that only the authorized user has access to its email box. If the identity of a user has to be certified, then the binding of a physical identity to a public key through a certificate must be performed by verifying the identity of the user itself. In an authentication mechanism based on the use of public certificates, the authenticator needs to get the claimant's certificate, which has been signed by some certification authority.

In a corporation network, it may happen that a user, it might be a human user or not, wishing to have access to the network, has no other access than the one for which it is asking access. This means that it has first had a contact with a system administrator or someone/something else to establish the common knowledge that is needed to authenticate. This first contact is usually a *personal contact*. This personal contact is actually needed for every kind of authentication type, from a simple password-based authentication method to a token card-based authentication method.

These issues become very important in case of public networks: how should such a personal contact happen, especially if a user is going to spend a limited amount of time there. One solution is to use a public network as a pass-through network, allowing a PPP tunnel to the user's home network. In this case the public network acts only as an access network and does not offer any service. If the services should be added on the network, in this case something more is needed, for allowing authentication, accounting and billing. A certificate-based authentication system could work quite well, but there are problems about how to manage certificates, trust of certification authorities and legal issues concerning billing. Obviously the user should have the certificate *before* accessing the networks, which might not be a trivial issue. A third solution may consist in creating different levels of trust: in each level the user might have certain rights and privileges, from only using the public network as a pass-through network to having complete access to all the services there available.

Appendix B: Structure of the implementation

This appendix describes very briefly the different functions that have been implemented in the prototype. It will not report all the code but only the aim of the various functions and the declaration of the classes.

B.1 Files common to both AP and MT

B.1.1 802_1Xv9.h

This files contains the basic declaration necessary for the implementation of the whole system. Format of an EAPOL packet and of a key-descriptor, different enumeration variable types, global variables and timers, port parameters, declaration of common classes, basic functions are all included here.

B.1.2 timer.cpp

Contains the implementation of the class performing the *Port Timers* state machine functionality, which is needed in both the supplicant and the authenticator. It has been implemented in the same way as described in the standard, although it could have been more effective if changed a little bit. The class has been declared as follows:

```
class TIMER {
      typedef enum _TIMER_STATE {TICK, ONE_SECOND} TIMER_STATE;

      //PRIVATE SYMBOLS

      //variables
      HANDLE h_timer_sm,h_timer_tick;          //handles to threads
      HANDLE h_timer_stop,h_tick_event,h_second;//handles to events
      TIMER_STATE state;                        //state

      //functions
      DWORD timer_sm(void);
      DWORD tick_gen(void);
      void dec(int* x);

      //friend functions
      friend DWORD __stdcall tick_start(void* pThreadParam);
      friend DWORD __stdcall sm_start(void* pThreadParam);


      //PUBLIC SYMBOLS
public:
      TIMER(void);
      ~TIMER(void);
      BOOL timer_start(void);
      void timer_stop(void);
};
```

B.1.3 generalFunc.cpp

Contains the implementation of some functions that are needed across the various files and that don't make use of the global symbols defined for that system, i.e. either the supplicant system or the authenticator system.

- *eapol_check_size()*: This function returns the size in bytes of an EAPOL packet that has to be sent over the network.
- *save_buffer_and_send()*: Takes the pointer of an EAPOL packet as a parameter, copies it in a temporary buffer and calls the function that interfaces with the network, which is *send_packet()*.
- *errorfunc()*: Deals with errors and sends a message to the user.

- *send_packet()*: Receives the length of the packet to be sent and a pointer to a buffer that stores the packet as parameters; prepares the Ethernet packet adding the source and destination address and sends it on the network.
- *set_size_eap_input()*: Returns the size of the EAP_INPUT structure used by the EAP API. It is necessary to identify the version of the APIs being used.
- *set_size_eap_info()*: Same as the previous function but with the EAP_INFO structure.
- *validate_EAPOL_packet()*: Finds out if a received EAPOL packet is valid and can be accepted as such by the PAEs. Checks the destination MAC address, the EAP Ethernet type and the EAPOL packet type.
- *receive_packets()*: This function is called by the network driver when an Ethernet frame is received. It saves the frame, validates it and saves it, and eventually sets an event in order to let another function to deal with the packet and perform the necessary actions.

B.1.4 globalFunc.cpp

Contains the implementation of functions that are needed across the files and that make use of global symbols. Its implementation changes a little bit between the supplicant's and authenticator's system, but the rationale behind them is the same.

- *monitor_packets()*: It's a thread that listens for events that indicate that a new valid EAPOL frame has been received. If it's the case, it analyzes the packet, finds out which kind of packet it is, and sets the necessary variables in the state machines.
- *setup_interface()*: Sets up and checks the state of the Ethernet interface.
- *stop_interface()*: Stops the Ethernet interface.

B.1.5 keyreceive.cpp

Contains the implementation of the *Key Receive* state machine, which is needed in both the supplicant's system and the authenticator's system. It performs the operation of dealing with a received EAPOL-Key packet and submits it to the right handler. Here its declaration:

```
class KEYRECEIVE {
        typedef enum _KEY_RECEIVE_STATE { NO_KEY_RECEIVE, KEY_RECEIVE}
            KEY_RECEIVE_STATE;

        KEY_RECEIVE_STATE state;
        P_KEY_DESCRIPTOR key;           //Pointer to a received key
        HANDLE h_keyrx_sleep, h_keyrx_stop, h_keyrx_sm;

        void processKey(void);
        BOOL eval_glob_trans();
        void keyrx_sm(void);

friend DWORD  __stdcall keyrx_start(void*pThreadparam);

public:
        BOOL rxKey;
        KEYRECEIVE(void);
        ~KEYRECEIVE(void);
};
```

B.2 Files only included in the MT

The following files are included only in the supplicant's system; they deal with the operation of the supplicant PAE, including the interface towards the EAP module.

B.2.1 supplicant.h

This files contains definitions of symbols and declarations of classes only needed in the supplicant's system. It is includes in all the files that are necessary on the MT side, and defines what can be called as the *supplicant's local environment*.

B.2.2 supplicant.cpp

Contains the implementation of the class that performs the *Supplicant* state machine functionality, and of all the functions that are necessary to its correct behavior, as defined in [8021X9]. Its declaration is the following:

```
class SUPPLICANT {
        typedef enum _SUPP_STATE { LOGOFF, DISCONNECTED,
                CONNECTING,ACQUIRED, AUTHENTICATING, HELD, AUTHENTICATED}
                SUPP_STATE;

        //PRIVATE VARIABLES USED IN THE SUPPLICANT CLASS

        SUPP_STATE state; //indicates the current state
        BOOL logoffSent;  //TRUE if a logoff message has been sent
        int startCount;   //counts the number of Start-packets being sent
        int previousId;   //Id of the previously sent EAP packet
        HANDLE h_supp_stop, h_supp_sleep, h_supp_sm; //handles to threads

        friend DWORD __stdcall supp_state_mach_start(void* pThreadParam);

        //PRIVATE FUNCTIONS
        void txStart(void);        //sends a Start packet
        void txLogoff(void);       //sends a Logoff packet
        void txRspId(BYTE, BYTE);  //sends an EAPOL/EAP-Resp/Id packet
        void txRspAuth(BYTE,BYTE); //sends an EAPOL/EAP (no Id) to Auth
        int supp_state_mach(void); //state machine
        BOOL eval_glob_trans(void);  //evaluates global transitions
public:
        //PUBLIC VARIABLES
        BOOL userLogoff; //set TRUE if the user is logged off
        BOOL reqId;      //set TRUE if an EAPOL/EAP-Req/Id is received
        BOOL reqAuth;    //set TRUE if EAPOL/EAP different than Req/Id is
received
        BOOL eapSuccess; //set TRUE if EAPOL/EAP/Success is received
        BOOL eapFail;    //set TRUE if EAOPOL/EAP/Failure is received

        //PUBLIC FUNCTIONS
        SUPPLICANT(void);          //constructor
        ~SUPPLICANT (void);        //destructor
        BOOL initializef(void);    //initializing function

};
```

B.2.3 maindll.cpp

This files contains all the different functions exported by the IEEE 802.1X module, implemented on the supplicant's system. Such functions are then called by the entity that loads the DLL. In the implemented system it will be the test program, that simulates the calls of the supervisor module.

• *setup()*: Prepares the supplicant's system; resources are allocated by this function in order to check if the authentication session can start.
• *start()*: Starts the authentication procedure, by activating the state machines.
• *stop()*: Stops the all the state machines implemented in the supplicant and deallocates resources.

- *suspend()*: Suspends temporarily the supplicant's state machines.
- *resume():* Resumes the state machines.
- *logon()*: Function that allows to set the value of the *userLogoff* variable, which indicates whether the user is logged on or not.
- *SetKeyTransEnabled()*: Allows to enable or disable the possibility to transmit a key.
- *KeyAvailable()*: Called when a new key is available. The key-descriptor is stored locally and then transmitted to the authenticator.
- *SetPortEnabledParameter()*: Used to change the value of the *portEnabled* parameter, which keeps track of the operational state of the port.

B.2.4 eapFunction.cpp

Contains functions needed for the interface to EAP, by using the EAP APIs on the supplicant's system. They are used to look up in the registry and setup the EAP APIs.

- *set_eap_input()*: prepares the *EapInput* structure, which has to be passed to the EAP APIs in each call.
- *readregister()*: reads in the register and stores locally the parameter needed for the EAP type being used.

B.2.5 supp_key_tran.cpp

Contains the implementation of the *Supplicant Key Transmit* state machine and the functions necessary for its management. Its declaration is as follows:

```
class SUPPLICANT_KEY_TRANSMIT {

        typedef enum _SUPP_KEY_TRAN_STATE { NO_SUPP_KEY_TRANSMIT,
            SUPP_KEY_TRANSMIT} SUPP_KEY_TRAN_STATE;

        SUPP_KEY_TRAN_STATE state;
        HANDLE h_supp_key_tran_sm, h_supp_key_tran_sleep,
            h_supp_key_tran_stop;

        BOOL eval_glob_trans(void);
        void supp_key_trans_sm();
        void txSuppKey(BYTE);

        friend DWORD __stdcall supp_key_tran_start(void *pThreadParam);

public:

        SUPPLICANT_KEY_TRANSMIT();
        ~SUPPLICANT_KEY_TRANSMIT();

        BOOL suppKeyAvailable;
};
```

B.3 Files only included in the AP

The following files are included in the authenticators module. They contain the functions necessary for its correct behaviour.

B.3.1 authenticator.h

Contains definitions and global symbols only needed in the authenticator's system. Furthermore it includes the declaration of the various classes used throughout this system and of some variables needed by the RADIUS client.

B.3.2 maindll.cpp

Contains functions exported by the IEEE 802.1X module implemented on the authenticator's system. They are called by the test program in order to simulate a normal behaviour of such a system.
- *setup()*: Setups the authenticator's system by initializing variables and allocating resources.
- *start()*: Starts the authenticator's state machines.
- *stop()*: Stops the state machines and allocates resources.
- *keyAvailable()*: Same function as in the supplicant's system.
- *SetDirection()*: Called to set the value of the *adminControlledDirection* parameter, which indicates what kind of control should be exerted over the controlled port, i.e. *Both* (blocking incoming and outcoming traffic to and from that port) or *In* (blocking only incoming traffic to that port).
- *SetPortEnabledParameter()*: Same function as in the supplicant's system.
- *SetKeyTransEnabled()*: Same function as in the supplicant's system.
- *GetAuthControlledPortStatus()*: Function used to read the status of the controlled port, after the authentication process has concluded.
- *SetControlledPortControl()*: Used to set the value of the *ControlledPortControl* parameter, in order to set which kind of control has to be exerted over the controlled port, i.e. *Auto* (port status set according to the authentication outcome), *ForceAuthorized* (port set to unconditionally to the *authorized* state), or *ForceUnauthorized* (port set unconditionally to the *unauthorized* state).
- *SetBridgeDetected()*: Used to set the value of the *bridgeDetected* parameter.

B.3.3 authenticator.cpp

Contains the implementation of the *Authenticator* state machine functionality and of other functions that are necessary for its correct behaviour. The class has been declared as follows:

```
class AUTHENTICATOR {

        typedef enum _AUTHENTICATOR_STATE { INITIALIZED, HELD,
            DISCONNECTED, CONNECTING, AUTHENTICATED, AUTHENTICATING,
            ABORTING, FORCE_AUTH,FORCE_UNAUTH } AUTHENTICATOR_STATE;

        //PRIVATE VARIABLES USED IN THE AUTHENTICATOR CLASS

        AUTHENTICATOR_STATE state;      //indicates the current state
        PORT_CONTROL portMode;
        int reAuthCount;  //times the CONNECTING state is entered

        HANDLE h_auth_stop;
        HANDLE h_auth_sm;
        HANDLE h_auth_sleep;

        friend DWORD __stdcall auth_sm_start(void* pThreadParam);

        //PRIVATE FUNCTIONS
        void txCannedFail(BYTE);        //sends a EAP/Failure to S
        void txCannedSuccess(BYTE);     //sends a EAP/Success packet to S
        void txReqId(BYTE);             //sends an EAP-Request/Identity to S
        void auth_sm(void);             //state machine
        BOOL eval_glob_trans(void);     //evaluates global transitions
        int latest_sent;

public:

        AUTHENTICATOR(void);    //Constructor
        ~AUTHENTICATOR(void);   //destructor
        BOOL inizializef(void);

        BOOL eapLogoff;
```

```
    BOOL eapStart;
    BOOL rxRespId;
};
```

B.3.4 authKeytrans.cpp

Contains the implementation of the *Authenticator Key Transmit* state machine, which deals with sending a key-descriptor to the supplicant.

```
class AUTHENTICATOR_KEY_TRANSMIT {

    typedef enum _AUTH_KEY_TRAN_STATE { NO_KEY_TRANSMIT,
        KEY_TRANSMIT} AUTH_KEY_TRAN_STATE;

    AUTH_KEY_TRAN_STATE state;
    HANDLE h_auth_key_tran_sm, h_auth_key_tran_sleep,
        h_auth_key_tran_stop;

    BOOL eval_glob_trans(void);
    void auth_key_trans_sm();
    void txKey(BYTE);

    friend DWORD __stdcall auth_key_tran_start(void *pThreadParam);

public:

    AUTHENTICATOR_KEY_TRANSMIT();          //constructor
    ~AUTHENTICATOR_KEY_TRANSMIT();         //destructor

    BOOL keyAvailable;
};
```

B.3.5 backend.cpp

Contains the implementation of the *Backend Authentication* state machine and related functions, which deals with the communication with the authentication server and the authentication function. The class has been declared as follows:

```
class BACKEND {

    typedef enum _BACKEND_STATE { INITIALIZED, IDLE, RESPONSE,
        SUCCEEDED, FAILED, TIMEOUT, REQUEST } BACKEND_STATE;

    //PRIVATE VARIABLES USED IN THE BACKEND CLASS

    BACKEND_STATE state;         //indicates the current state
    int reqCount;//numbers of EAP/Request packs sent without response
    HANDLE h_back_stop;
    HANDLE h_back_sm;            //handles to threads
    HANDLE h_back_sleep;

    friend DWORD __stdcall backend_state_mach_start(void*
        pThreadParam);

    //PRIVATE FUNCTIONS
    void txReq(BYTE);            //sends a EAP/Request packet to S
    void SendRespToServer(void); //sends a EAP/Response packet to AS
    void txSuccess(BYTE);        //sends  an EAP/Success Packet to S
    void txFail(BYTE);           //sends  an EAP/Fail Packet to S
```

```
        void abortAuth(void);          //releases resources after authent.
        void backend_state_mach(void);//state machine
        void backtxCannedFail(BYTE);   //sends an EAP/Failed pac. to S
        BOOL eval_glob_trans(void);    //evaluates global transitions
        int latest_sent;
public:
        //PUBLIC FUNCTIONS
        BOOL aSuccess;      //set TRUE if EAP/Sucess packet is received
        BOOL aFail;         //set TRUE if EAP/Fail is received
        BOOL aReq;          //set TRUE if EAP/Request is received from AS
        int idFromServer;   //id of the most recent EAP pac. received
        BACKEND(void);        //constructor
        ~BACKEND (void);      //destructor
        BOOL initializef(void); //initializing function

        //PUBLIC VARIABLES
        BOOL rxResp;        //set TRUE if EAP pack. is received from S.
};
```

B.3.6 contrDir.cpp

Contains the implementation of the *Controlled Directions* state machine and the functions needed for its correct use.

```
class CONTROL_DIRECTIONS {

        typedef enum _CONTR_DIR_STATE {FORCE_BOTH, IN_OR_BOTH}
            CONTR_DIR_STATE;

        CONTR_DIR_STATE state;
        HANDLE h_con_dir_sleep, h_con_dir_stop, h_con_dir_sm;

        BOOL eval_glob_trans(void);
        void con_dir_sm();

        friend DWORD __stdcall con_dir_start(void* pThreadParam);

public:

        CONTROL_DIRECTIONS(void);      //constructor
        ~CONTROL_DIRECTIONS (void);    //destructor

        DIRECTIONS operControlledDirections;
};
```

B.3.7 reauthen.cpp

Contains the implementation of the *Reauthentication* state machine. The class has been declared as follows:

```
class REAUTHENTICATION {

        typedef enum _REAUTH_STATE { INITIALIZED, REAUTHENTICATE}
            REAUTH_STATE;

        REAUTH_STATE state;
        HANDLE h_reauth_sleep, h_reauth_stop, h_reauth_sm;

        BOOL eval_glob_trans();
        void reauth_sm(void);
```

```
friend DWORD __stdcall reauth_start_sm(void *pThreadParam);

public:
      REAUTHENTICATION(void);        //constructor
      ~REAUTHENTICATION(void);       //destructor
};
```

B.3.8 RADIUSfuncs.cpp

Contains the functions related to the RADIUS protocol and the communication with the RADIUS server as well as the management of the ActiveX control that implements the client.

- *RADIUS_setup()*: Starts the RADIUS client, by instantiating a COM object, getting the pointers to its interfaces and getting the methods that are needed later on.
- *RADIUS_send_and_receive()*: Prepares a RADIUS packet, encapsulates an EAP packet in it, sends it to the server, retrieves the answer and saves the received EAP packet in a locally allocated memory area..

Appendix C: The usage of the Microsoft EAP APIs

This appendix aims to give an overview about how the Microsoft EAP APIs have to be used in order to establish and control an EAP protocol exchange. Assuming to have the rights to make use of such APIs, it is possible to establish a complete EAP communication without ever building an EAP packet, except for the packets used to request and state one's identity, which have to be created manually. This is due to the fact that such APIs were thought to be used by the RAS client and server, when requesting and granting access to a remote network: in this situation the identity of the authenticate is known through a different channel.

C.1 Looking up in the registry

Before using the EAP APIs, the DLL corresponding to the desired EAP method, which implements the authentication scheme that will be used, must be installed on the system. In order to know which EAP-types are installed, it is possible to check the following registry keys:
HKEY_LOCAL_MACHINE\System\CurrentControlSet\Services\Rasman\PPP\EAP\<eap_type_id>, where *<eap_type_id>* indicates the EAP-type assigned number. Having chosen one of the available methods, it is necessary to retrieve some configuration information stored in the registry under the appropriate key. Many EAP types might be available within the same DLL: for this reason each call to one of the methods implemented in a DLL must include as a parameter the EAP-type number, which is referred in the call.

The information in the registry include the path of the DLL (*Path*) implementing the authentication scheme, the friendly name of the EAP method (*FriendlyName*), if the programmer must call the standard Windows user-name dialog or a specific UI for getting information about the user's identity and password (*InvokeUsernameDialog* and *InvokePasswordDialog*), and the path to the DLL that implements the user interface if available (*IdentityPath*). Furthermore it might happen that the specific authentication method requires preliminary configuration by the user before being used (*RequireConfigUI*); in this case a DLL implements the interface for it and its path can be retrieved from the registry (*ConfigUIPath*); some configuration data might be stored in the registry as well (*DafaultData*). If configuration is needed also on the server side, then the registry stores the CLSID of the object implementing such an interface (*ConfigCLSID*). For some EAP method, the user might be required to provide further information during the authentication exchange; in this case the registry stores the path to the DLL that implements this interactive UI (*InteractiveUIPath*). Finally, it is possible to know from the registry if the EAP method supports encryption-keys exchange (*MPPEEncryptionSupported*) and if it can be used on standalone Windows 2000 machines (*StandaloneSupported*) or if it needs an external authentication provider.

C.2 Setting up the EAP APIs

The DLL that implements an EAP-type exports basically only one method, *RasEapGetInfo()*, which allows to retrieve information about the other methods that need to be called during the protocol exchange. The function receives two parameters: the EAP-type number (*dwEapTypeId*), in order to distinguish between different methods implemented in the same DLL and the pointer to a structure called PPP_EAP_INFO. This structure will be filled in by the called method with the addresses of the methods later called by the user of the EAP APIs. Such methods are: *RasEapInitialize()*, *RasEapBegin()*, *RasEapEnd()*, and *RasEapMakeMessage()*. In case of error, an error code will be returned by the call, specifying the problem.

To start EAP, it is necessary to call the function *RasEapInitialize()*, which prepares the APIs. It receives the EAP-type as a parameter and a flag stating if it is called to start or to stop the EAP APIs (fInitialize); this function has indeed to be called at the beginning and at the end of the authentication session, to start and to dismiss the API's. Such function might not be implemented if no initialization operations are needed.

C.3 Configuration and start up

It might happen that on the client side an EAP method needs to be configured before being used the first time. Such configuration information are not *user-dependant* but *machine-dependant*. If this is the case (the registry variable *RequireConfigUI* is set to 1), a DLL stored on the system implements a method called *RasEapInvokeConfigUI()*, which provides for the configuration UI. This method is not called by the programmer using the EAP APIs but usually by the Dial-In Network Manager, provided by the Windows 2000 RAS client. These information are stored together with other system-dependant information by the RAS manager and are retrieved before starting an EAP session. A programmer wishing to use an EAP method that needs configuration information must retrieve and pass them to the APIs. In the achieved implementation, this aspect has not been considered since the method used for testing purpose did not require any previous settings; a complete implementation, wishing to use the EAP APIs made available by the Windows OS, should deal with that aspect: it should be able to configure an EAP method, store the configuration information and retrieve them when necessary. As an alternative, it is also possible to retrieve the information from the RAS network manager or from the phone book, where they also might be stored.

In order to free the memory area allocated for the configuration information, the programmer has to call the *RasEapFreeMemory*() method, implemented in the same DLL as the configuration UI; this should happen after the information have been passed to the EAP APIs, i.e. after the call to *RasEapBegin*.

User-dependant information should instead be retrieved through the identity functions, described later on. Furthermore, the EAP API's might request the user (RAS manager or a programmer) to store further information in the registry during the authentication exchange, by passing a pointer to it at the return from a call to the function *RasEapMakeMessage*(), used in the protocol exchange and described in the next Section.

Before starting a protocol exchange, it is necessary to retrieve user information. This might be accomplished by calling the standard Windows user-name dialog (if the registry value *InvokeUserDialog* is set to 1) or by invoking a method made available by the EAP DLL, called *RasEapGetIdentity*(), which implements a customized user interface. Information retrieved in such a way should then be passed to the EAP APIs; later the memory allocated in order to store them, should be freed by calling *RasEapFreeMemory*(), as happens for configuration information. A pointer to the user information is passed to the functions *RasEapBegin*() and *RasEapMakeMessage*().

In order to allow a successful EAP authentication, the APIs need some information that are passed to them through the call *RasEapBegin*(). The protocol, i.e. the authentication method, allocates a buffer whose pointer is then passed back to the caller, who has to store it and include it as a parameter at each call of the method *RasEapMakeMessage*().The function receives furthermore a pointer to a structure of type PPP_EAP_INPUT, containing information about the user (name, password if on the client's side, if it's the client or the server side, etc), the expected EAP ID Code, and, if on the server's side, a structure containing a set of attributes, later needed for the connection. It is worth to point out again that the original aim of the Windows EAP API's was to be used for authentication by the RAS client and the RAS server, while accessing a remote network, not by a common user or a programmer. For this reason certain aspects were quite difficult to exploit or to use correctly.

C.4 Message Exchange

In order to state the EAP conversation, the function *RasEapMakeMessage*() must be called on both the client's and the server's side. The function will be passed the last EAP message received from the other party; the first call will contain an empty message, to start the conversation. On return from the call, the caller will receive a structure of type PPP_EAP_OUTPUT, which will indicate the action that has to be taken in order to go on with the conversation.

If a new EAP packet has to be sent to the other party, one of the following values will be returned: EAP_ACTION_Send, EAP_ACTION_SendAndDone, EAP_ACTION_SendWithTimeout, EAP_ACTION_SendWithTimeoutInteractive. The packet to be sent will be one of the members of the PPP_EAP_OUTPUT structure. The authentication protocol returns also the expected ID of the next packet. If the ID does not match, the packet has to be discarded.

If the action is either EAP_ACTION_SendAndDone or EAP_ACTION_Done the protocol exchange can be considered concluded. The caller should also check the value of the *dwAuthResultCode* member for getting the outcome of the authentication process. The authentication protocol may also return a structure containing some attributes about the connection (*pUserAttributes*).

There are some situations in which the actual authentication is not performed by the EAP method but by some external authentication provider. In this case, the *RasEapMakeMessage*() methods returns the value EAP_ACTION_Authenticate, which triggers the call of an external authentication provider.

If the caller comes to know that authentication has successfully completed in some other way than through the APIs, it will inform the APIs in the next call to the *RasEapMakeMessage*(). If the interactive UI has to be called during the authentication exchange, a flag in the PPP_EAP_OUTPUT structure will be set.

At the end of the protocol exchange, when the outcome of the authentication exchange has been found out, the function *RasEapEnd*() needs to be called, in order to allow the EAP APIs to free the allocated resources.

YOUR KNOWLEDGE HAS VALUE

- We will publish your bachelor's and
  master's thesis, essays and papers

- Your own eBook and book -
  sold worldwide in all relevant shops

- Earn money with each sale

Upload your text at www.GRIN.com
and publish for free

GRIN